There is no shortage of talent, skill, and desire to contribute to research among academics at teaching-intensive universities. The shortages are pragmatic—not enough time and resources. This highly-engaging book tackles these barriers head-on with effective strategies and practical advice.

—**Brian Nosek, University of Virginia, USA**

Two experienced professors provide an invaluable road map for navigating the challenges of successfully conducting research at colleges and universities that primarily focus on teaching.

—**Jonathan Schooler, University of California,**
Santa Barbara, USA

Combining a heavy teaching load with a flourishing research program can be challenging. In a clear, engaging way, this book offers practical guidelines for college teachers on how to succesfully set up a research line.

—**Susan Branje, Utrecht University, The Netherlands**

Both authors have done it! Treating us to personal experiences, they take us enjoyably and clearly through the problems and solutions, leaving us knowing how—in unpromising circumstances—we could do it too.

—**Kate Miriam Loewenthal, Royal Holloway,**
University of London, UK

The strategies for balancing teaching and research along with the discussion of job satisfaction makes this book a must-read for graduate students making decisions about job applications, assistant professors just getting started and senior professors looking for inspiration.

—**Katherine Jewsbury Conger, University of California,**
Davis, USA

LAUNCHING A SUCCESSFUL RESEARCH PROGRAM AT A TEACHING UNIVERSITY

This practical guide addresses the challenges for building and maintaining a college research program in an environment that does not focus on supporting research activity and for those with a heavy teaching load. The challenges faced by teacher-researchers and solutions to issues are reviewed. The steps for maximizing research productivity are outlined: time management, obtaining research space and equipment and funding, recruiting and managing human subjects, and overcoming bureaucratic stumbling blocks. Chapters feature opening vignettes, examples, cases, figures, tables, summaries, suggested readings, and research references which provide a scientific grounding.

Highlights include coverage of:
- The latest time-saving digital resources including automatic literature search alerts, Zotero for managing literature, Dropbox for sharing files, Open Science for managing workflow, and OpenSesame and OpenStax Tutor.
- Strategies for recruiting subjects such as flyers and posting lab meeting minutes on a web page.
- How to increase research productivity while still engaging in effective teaching.
- The problems of the availability of human subjects and strategies for recruiting from classes, offering extra credit for research participation, and participation as a course requirement.
- Using students as volunteer research assistants and strategies for recruiting and managing volunteers along with ethical considerations.
- Bureaucratic stumbling blocks and strategies for overcoming those challenges.
- How to use browser/word processor add-ons that store and organize literature in a searchable library and produce citations and reference lists.
- The use of free open source software to design experiments and collect data and free cloud-based resources to store electronic research files.

Intended for professional development or teacher training courses offered in masters and doctoral programs in colleges and universities or as a supplement in graduate level research methods courses, this book is also an invaluable resource for faculty development centers and university administrators. Designed for both early career and veteran teacher-researchers looking to enhance their research productivity, this book appeals to college teachers of all levels and disciplines.

Robert S. Ryan is an Associate Professor of Psychology at Kutztown University of Pennsylvania.

Avidan Milevsky is an Associate Professor of Psychology and Director of the Center for Parenting Research at Ariel University in Israel.

LAUNCHING A SUCCESSFUL RESEARCH PROGRAM AT A TEACHING UNIVERSITY

Robert S. Ryan
Avidan Milevsky

Routledge
Taylor & Francis Group

NEW YORK AND LONDON

First published 2017
by Routledge
711 Third Avenue, New York, NY 10017

and by Routledge
2 Park Square, Milton Park, Abingdon, Oxon, OX14 4RN

Routledge is an imprint of the Taylor & Francis Group, an informa business

Library of Congress Cataloging-in-Publication Data

Names: Ryan, Robert S., author. | Milevsky, Avidan, author.
Title: Launching a successful research program at a teaching university / Robert S. Ryan, Ph.D., Avidan Milevsky, Ph.D.
Description: New York, NY: Routledge, 2017.
Identifiers: LCCN 2016010828| ISBN 9781138638877 (hardback: alk. paper) |
ISBN 9781138638884 (pbk.: alk. paper) | ISBN 9781315516578 (ebk)
Subjects: LCSH: College teachers—Workload. | Research—Management. | College teaching. | Education, Higher—Research. | Learning and scholarship.
Classification: LCC LB2331 .R86 2017 | DDC 378.1/25—dc23LC
record available at https://lccn.loc.gov/2016010828

ISBN: 978-1-138-63887-7 (hbk)
ISBN: 978-1-138-63888-4 (pbk)
ISBN: 978-1-315-51657-8 (ebk)

Typeset in Bembo
by codeMantra

To the two people who most make my life worth living and whose sacrifices have enabled me to achieve my dreams: My daughters April and Laura.

—RSR

To our past department chair, Dr. Anita Meehan, for the years of encouragement and support.

—AM

CONTENTS

PREFACE

Congratulations! You trekked your way through more than eight years of school. After a grueling undergraduate education, applying to graduate schools, being rejected by many and accepted by few, years of graduate work, a master's thesis and maybe even a doctoral dissertation you have finally reached the point where you are ready to apply for professorships. After many applications, tracking down old transcripts, and submitting all materials, you secured several job interviews. Traveling, staying in cheap hotels, and interviewing with department chairs and many committees and now you finally secured your first academic position. After a summer of moving and settling into your new place you find yourself at the end of the first week of your first semester of being a professor. You feel you could barely keep up with the amount of work that's coming up with preparing and teaching your classes. But then the thought crosses your mind, you need to get going on your research agenda. You ask yourself, "Now what?"

You've been teaching for quite some time at a liberal arts college or at an institution focused on teaching as you begin hearing from colleagues across the institution that the administration is slowly beginning to focus more on your professional development credentials in making promotion decisions. Although you tried engaging in some research over the years, the burdens of teaching three to four courses a semester have limited your presentation and publication output. You think to yourself that there is no way you could launch now a thriving and successful research career considering the amount of time you are spending just on your teaching and committee responsibilities. You ask yourself, "Now what?"

This book is intended to answer the question of "Now what?"

Several recent developments offer faculty resources to get the most out of their research while balancing teaching and service responsibilities. For example, developments in digital technology have provided time and labor saving resources that can be especially helpful to faculty who are looking to maximize their productivity. Highlighting some of these resources, this book offers specific suggestions on how to launch and increase research productivity while being able to engage in effective teaching.

The book also addresses the solutions to the kinds of nuts and bolts problems that researchers encounter in institutions increasingly requiring research productivity with little financial and instrumental support.

Each chapter begins with an introduction including specific bullets about what the reader will either understand or learn in each of the chapters and an overview of the material covered. The book's narrative is peppered with specific examples and cases helping the reader to apply the information. The book includes specific research highlights and references that offer a scientific grounding for the material. Chapters include figures and tables that assist in delineating several aspects of the material. Each chapter concludes with a summary and several suggested readings to further your understanding and information about the topics covered.

The book highlights five specific areas of focus and offers detailed descriptions of what could be done to enhance and maximize productivity in each of these five areas. The five areas of focus are: managing time more effectively, learning how to obtain research space, equipment, and other resources, understanding and navigating the availability of human subjects, utilizing undergraduate research assistance to be part of your research efforts, and finally understanding how to navigate the many bureaucratic stumbling blocks common in university systems. In highlighting the solutions for the five impediments, the book emphasizes the latest digital resources that can be used in accomplishing the stated goals. For example, the book includes descriptions of some of the latest time-saving digital resources. These include automatic literature search alerts, Zotero for managing your literature, Dropbox for sharing files with research assistants, the Open Science Framework for managing all aspects of your workflow, and putting lab meeting notes on a website. The book also deals with logistical concerns and solutions such as how to obtain space, equipment, and other resources. For example, the book discusses strategies involved in obtaining funding. The book also provides specific examples illustrating how different research methods can make use of the limited resources that may be available at the beginning of a program so as to build a case for asking for more resources to expand a program. For example, the book describes OpenSesame, an open source platform for building experiments to be presented via computer. Other logistical issues covered are issues of availability of human subjects including a description of the advantages and disadvantages of methods such as ad hoc recruiting from classes, offering extra credit for research participation, participation as a course requirement, and motivating students to participate in research as subjects. Furthermore, the book offers managerial information as well as addressing issues of utilizing undergraduates as volunteer research assistants. It presents two alternative methods that we call the "exclusive club" and the "open door" method. The book presents strategies for advertising, recruiting, managing, and delegating including specific examples of materials, such as flyers, and innovative techniques, such as recording lab meeting minutes as a web page. The book also discusses issues relating to the logistics of taking students to conferences.

Combined, an understanding of these five areas will help faculty members increase their research productivity ultimately leading them to the eventual goal of achieving academic job satisfaction.

This book is intended for both an early career professor who is looking to launch a successful research career and someone who has been teaching for some time and is now looking to be able to be productive on the research front even with a full teaching load. As such, it is also ideal for professional development or teacher training courses offered in masters and doctoral programs in colleges and universities, as well as an invaluable resource for faculty development centers, college and university administrators looking to improve teaching at their institutions. The book may also serve as a useful supplement in graduate level research methods courses.

It will appeal to faculty members in diverse areas using different methodologies. One of the main reasons that we are collaborating on this book is precisely because both of us have succeeded in developing a productive research program in diverse areas of content and methodology. Dr. Milevsky's work is in socioemotional development and his methodology is mainly qualitative. Dr. Ryan's work focuses on cognitive processes and is quantitative. Thus, by working together we were able to produce a book with a wide appeal to faculty in varied disciplines.

We would like to conclude with thanking the many people who were invaluable in the development of this book. Debra Riegert, Senior Editor, and Rachel Severinovsky, Editorial Assistant and the entire team at Routledge for their efforts and support. We would also like to thank the reviewers who provided us with valuable feedback on the book including Colette Cann from Vassar College and one anonymous reviewer. Dr. Michele Baranczyk of Kutztown University of Pennsylvania contributed the idea of using an LMS as a platform for collecting data, as described in Chapter 3. Dr. Bruce Warner, formerly of Kutztown University of Pennsylvania and now at Pittsburg State University in Kansas contributed the idea that the difficulty of bureaucratic stumbling blocks can be eased by gradually educating administrators about the difficulties faced by faculty trying to conduct research at a teaching institution, as described in Chapter 6. Finally, we thank our colleagues in the psychology department at Kutztown University of Pennsylvania, including department chair Dr. Gregory Shelley, for creating an environment of support and cordiality conducive for professional growth and development.

ABOUT THE AUTHORS

Dr. Robert S. Ryan is an Associate Professor of Psychology at Kutztown University of Pennsylvania. Most recently he has been teaching experimental methods and statistics for the social and behavioral sciences almost exclusively. Previously, he has taught theories of learning, learning motivation and emotion, cognitive psychology, and general psychology, as well as special topics courses on consciousness, foundations of psychology, and independent research. He has extensive experience integrating research into classes, conducting research in a lab, and has conducted research on the Internet.

Dr. Ryan has published five peer-reviewed journal articles, two of the more recent of which have Kutztown University undergraduate students as co-authors. One of those demonstrates the feasibility of using the Internet to conduct research.

Most recently, he was a contributing author to the Open Science Collaboration's Reproducibility Project: Psychology, which was published in the journal *Science*. Also, he is a co-author on one published book chapter. Finally, he has presented 36 various posters and talks at local, regional, national, and international conferences. Of those, a total of 34 different Kutztown University undergraduate students served as co-authors on 14 of them.

Dr. Avidan Milevsky is an Associate Professor of Psychology at Ariel University in Israel. He serves as the director of the Center for Parenting Research at AU. His work on families, parenting, and siblings has produced over 100 papers, over 20 peer-reviewed articles, and 5 books including *Sibling Relationships in Childhood and Adolescence: Predictors and Outcomes* by Columbia University Press.

1
INTRODUCTION

After Reading This Chapter You Will Understand

- The main objectives of this book
- The five typical challenges faced by faculty looking to engage in effective teaching and productive research
- The way the current book responds to each of these five challenges

Introduction

You decided to read this book for one of two reasons. First, you are a new faculty member and are trying to figure out how to combine being effective in your teaching with establishing a thriving research program.

Alternatively, you may find yourself in a different situation. You may have been teaching for many years already and you are slowly learning that in order to advance even in teaching institutions you may need to enhance your research productivity (Fairweather, 2005). You may be looking for some guidance on how to continue your teaching effectiveness while growing your research efforts.

Being both an effective teacher and productive researcher require effort and creativity. This book is going to teach you many techniques to be able to streamline both your teaching and your research, thus producing a healthy, and fruitful, balance between the two. However, this book is not just about learning how to balance a full teaching load and a productive research program. This book is ultimately about job satisfaction.

The Book's Objective

The field of organizational theory has produced over the years a considerable amount of research on job satisfaction (Cranny, Smith, & Stone, 1992). However, research on job satisfaction in academia is relatively limited (Terpstra & Honoree, 2004). There are several elements that are known about broader job satisfaction that have been applied to our understanding of job satisfaction in academia.

Job satisfaction has been viewed from economic, psychological, sociological, and ethnographic viewpoints (Bozeman & Gaughan, 2011). In an attempt to find some parsimony in job satisfaction research, several theoretical propositions have suggested that job satisfaction can be categorized into two broader components—one being intrinsic job satisfaction and the other being extrinsic job satisfaction (Kalleberg, 1977; Seifert & Umbach, 2008). Intrinsic job satisfaction is the extent to which the work engaged in is self-motivating, interesting, enlightening, and internally satisfying. On the other hand, extrinsic job satisfaction is driven by external aspects of the job which may ultimately lead to satisfaction. These external aspects include financial related arrangements such as salary, benefits, and a sense of having a secure job. Furthermore, extrinsic satisfaction may be derived from social opportunities that the job offers such as relationships with co-workers.

In truth, although the intrinsic versus extrinsic job satisfaction dichotomy helps in offering an organized view on job satisfaction more broadly, in practice, intrinsic and extrinsic dimensions of job satisfaction constantly interact (Bozeman & Gaughan, 2011). For example, when an academic publishes a paper in a prestigious journal, which usually would produce a sense of job satisfaction, this satisfaction entails both intrinsic and extrinsic dimensions. Intrinsically, there is a sense of satisfaction of having produced an exceptional piece of writing. However, there are also extrinsic advantages to the publication as it may assist in promotion and ultimately higher pay.

Studies on job satisfaction in academia have highlighted several factors that may impact both intrinsic and extrinsic job satisfaction. For example, a considerable literature exists on gender differences in job satisfaction among university faculty members. Studies have shown that females consistently report lower job satisfaction than males (Sabharwal & Corley, 2009; Seifert & Umbach, 2008; Turner, 2002; Turner & Myers, 2000). Additionally, studies have also shown race to be a factor in job satisfaction. Studies have indicated that faculty of color report lower job satisfaction than white faculty members (Rockquemore & Laszloffy, 2008). Research has also shown that academic job satisfaction may also be a function of geographic region (Gabbidon & Higgins, 2012). Other non-demographic factors that may impact job satisfaction include level of autonomy at work, type of discipline, marital and family status, rank, pay, and even religiosity (Bozeman & Gaughan, 2011; Gabbidon & Higgins, 2012; Hagedorn, 2000; Watson, Storey, Wynarczyk, Keasey, & Short, 1996). Having greater autonomy, working in the hard sciences, being married and having children, being tenured and promoted, receiving higher wages, and self-reporting of religious belief and involvement have all been shown to be related to job satisfaction.

Regardless of all these factors, studies are pretty clear that working with limited job satisfaction is linked with stress, burnout, seeking other jobs in academia, and ultimately leaving academia altogether (Hagedorn, 1996; Rosser, 2004). On the other hand, elevated job satisfaction is associated with better mental and physical health and with overall life satisfaction (Cranny, Smith, & Stone, 1992).

Examining the aggregate information from all the indicated factors that may contribute to job satisfaction in academia, two overarching factors have been highlighted as the main elements in determining job satisfaction in academia: research productivity and having a healthy work/life balance (Bozeman & Gaughan, 2011; Gabbidon & Higgins, 2012).

This brings us to the objective of this book. Knowing how to streamline both your teaching and research work by managing time, using all available resources, and utilizing a growing reservoir of electronic tools for both teaching and research, will lead to greater productivity and better time and work management. This will ultimately produce greater job satisfaction.

The Five Typical Challenges

Taking into account the importance of productivity and finding a healthy balance between home and work, there are five specific areas that faculty members could focus on in creating an environment that is conducive to personal achievement. The five areas are: time management issues, obtaining space, equipment, and other resources, issues of the availability of human subjects, using undergraduate students as research assistants, and bureaucratic stumbling blocks common in university systems.

Time Constraints

People think that with the limited hours of actual teaching, faculty members must have an abundant amount of time to focus on all areas of their career and home life. However, when taking into account the amount of time it takes to prepare for classes, review class material, grade papers and tests, work individually with students during office hours and beyond, together with the growing importance of committee work and the hours spent on sitting through committee meetings, in addition to post-committee work, coupled with attempting to grow a research program, at the end of the day faculty members find themselves constrained by time. This often leads to necessitating staying extra hours in the evenings or even engaging in work over the weekends.

Particularly if you are an early career academic just the amount of time you need to spend preparing for class may prevent you from being able to engage in any meaningful research.

If you are employed by a liberal arts college or a university focused more on teaching, you may be teaching three or even four courses a semester. This may translate into between 12 and 15 hours of classroom time. Add to this the several hours you need to prepare for each hour of classroom instruction together with grading papers, preparing exams, and grading exams, and you may find very little time for other activities. An additional consideration is that in teaching institutions you may be teaching large sections of the course with little assistance from graduate students. In more of the larger research institutions, faculty members often utilize the help of graduate teaching assistants for a lot of the extra class work including grading and other administrative work. However, at schools with limited graduate programs, faculty members need to find creative ways of streamlining their work to be able to manage classroom time and have the ability of engaging in meaningful research as well.

Needing to keep up with all the necessary work produces a considerable amount of time pressure. This tension contributes to work-related stress, minimizes productivity, and ultimately infringes on the healthy balance between work and family. Having specific suggestions in order to manage time more productively can go a long way in minimizing work stress, increasing productivity, and enhancing job satisfaction.

Obtaining Space, Equipment, and Other Resources

A second area of focus that can assist in increasing productivity and managing the overall balance of work and home is knowing the ins and outs of obtaining research space, equipment, and other resources to engage in a productive research program. It is not always clear at the get go how exactly space, equipment, and resources are obtained. Although these issues may be peripherally discussed during an academic job interview, the realities of the situation may not become evident until the job actually begins.

As the first couple of weeks and months of an academic career begin, it becomes even more evident that obtaining research space, equipment, and resources requires some effort. Part of the process requires knowing how to navigate the university system in order to obtain the necessary research space, equipment, and many other resources in order to launch a productive research program. Often the lack of clarity on these issues can create work-related stress which ultimately will interfere with overall productivity and will impair job satisfaction.

On the other hand, possessing the right type of research space and equipment can help streamline your research making it more productive. In addition to having space to store your materials and your equipment, having work space offers your research students, as discussed in Chapter 5, a place for them to conduct research, collect data, enter data, and engage in various other lab-related tasks. Having a designated space for students to work on your research adds a level of authority and importance to your research which, in turn, motivates students to engage more fervently in your research.

Having the information necessary, understanding the ins and outs of obtaining research space, equipment, and other resources, and minimizing the time spent on navigating the system by streamlining the process will all be helpful for engaging in a productive research program.

This will ultimately produce greater job satisfaction.

Availability of Human Subjects

A third area of information necessary in order to engage in a productive research program leading to greater job satisfaction is issues relating to the availability and access to human subjects. This is particularly relevant in disciplines that utilize human subjects for research such as social work, criminal justice, psychology, counseling, and education. You may have some great ideas in terms of research questions to investigate; however, if you do not have access to human subjects for data collection all these ideas will ultimately remain as ideas. Decisions about the areas of research to engage in need to take into account both personal interests and the realities of the availability of the subjects necessary for your ideas.

It may often actually be the first step you take in determining the trajectory of your research plan. Begin by thinking about the potential availability of human subjects or samples and then based on the availability you can massage your overall interests in order for them to fit into the types of samples you have the ability of securing. It can often be very frustrating for faculty members who have great research questions and plans to then get stuck when they are trying to figure out where to actually find participants.

In order to be able to engage in a productive research program you will have to have specific information about how to access human subjects and the best practices in collecting data using human subjects. Having specific information and tips about where to access and how to navigate data collection with human subjects will go a long way in creating a productive research program which ultimately will lead to greater job satisfaction.

Using Undergraduates as Volunteer Research Assistants

A fourth area of focus that can be extremely beneficial in creating a productive research program is knowing how to utilize undergraduate students as a research assistant. This is particularly relevant for faculty members teaching in liberal arts colleges or other universities that have smaller graduate programs and many undergraduate students. The lack of graduate students with research assistantship or graduate assistantships does not mean that the entire burden of research has to lay on you. Undergraduate students can be an extremely valuable resource.

In fact, the research trajectory I have taken started with an area of inquiry that I embarked on as an undergraduate student. Considering that the program I was in during my undergraduate years did not have faculty members who were offering research opportunities for undergraduate students, I had to reach out to a different university in the area in order to be able to find a research mentor who was interested in an undergraduate student research assistant. My mentor was willing to integrate me into all aspects of her research work as a junior in college. I found this opportunity refreshing and I was able to devote a considerable amount of time during my third and fourth year of undergraduate education on this research. After graduation I did my graduate work at this institution and I continued working with my mentor throughout my masters and doctoral work. This is a great example of how the right type of undergraduate student can be extremely productive in research work. Knowing how to identify and train undergraduate students in your research work can offer an invaluable asset in your overall research agenda.

Having specific information and concrete ideas about how to engage undergraduate students in your research could go a long way in helping your research goals. This student involvement will ultimately offer you valuable work and will free up your time to focus on areas of research that only you could engage in and will also free up your time to being able to apply yourself to other job requirements. Knowing how to effectively work and utilize undergraduate students as research assistants will help in your research productivity, will minimize your workday stress, and will ultimately lead to greater job satisfaction.

Bureaucratic Stumbling Blocks

Finally, an area of information that can be very beneficial in your objectives is knowing how to deal with bureaucratic stumbling blocks common in university systems. Taking the time in learning, upfront, what can be done in navigating these issues will minimize the amount of time that is usually spent in trying to the deal with the stumbling blocks when they are faced. Furthermore, considering the research that highlights how some of these bureaucratic dynamics of universities are linked with job dissatisfaction and heightened stress (Gabbidon & Higgins, 2012), learning now how to navigate the stumbling blocks will lead to minimizing stress and elevating job satisfaction and productivity.

University faculties are notorious for having many members who are continuously disgruntled by the system. I have found that these individuals may have had great plans when they originally joined the faculty but as they began navigating the university system and some of the bureaucracy inherent in large educational institutions they slowly developed the bitterness that affected and infected all aspects of their work. Knowing ahead of time what to expect can minimize the likelihood of you turning out like one of those unhappy members of academia.

Book Overview

The upcoming chapters will be devoted to each of these five areas and will suggest specific ways to tackle the difficulties inherent in each of these five categories. The next five chapters will each tackle one of these five issues with specific tips, suggestions, and examples to be applied immediately in enhancing your research productivity, minimizing work-based stress, and enhancing your job satisfaction. The upcoming five chapters will offer specific information to help in time management, obtaining space, equipment, and other resources, how to tap into and navigate human subjects, how to utilize the great resource of undergraduates as research assistants, and how to confront common bureaucratic stumbling blocks of the university environment.

Taken together, the focus of the upcoming five chapters on these five broad categories of information will offer faculty members a specific and concrete track in developing and maintaining an active, vibrant, and productive research program. Coupled with streamlining and managing time, the upcoming chapters will impact not only your productivity but your overall work–life balance, producing less job base stress and elevated job satisfaction.

Chapter Overview

In the next chapter we will describe strategies to overcome the first of the five difficulties—time constraints. For example, we explain the importance of not being discouraged early because developing a research program will take more time than at a research university. However, your patience will pay off. We then describe the steps involved in building a program and strategies to be more efficient. For example, we will describe the Overlapping Independent Studies Strategies, a way to enable the researcher to run subjects in one study while working on other aspects of a different study, such as preparations or data analysis. Also, several different strategies for increasing teaching efficiency will be described in detail. This chapter will include descriptions of some of the latest time-saving digital resources as well. These will include automatic literature search alerts, Zotero for managing your literature, Dropbox for sharing files with research assistants, the Open Science Framework for managing all aspects of your workflow, and putting lab meeting notes on a website. It will also include a brief description of two other resources, OpenSesame and OpenStax Tutor, along with a note that each will be described in more detail in later chapters as we come to the functions to which they can be applied. It will also note that our treatment of all of these resources should be considered to be merely an entry point into a potentially vast invaluable area, but one that is a moving target because these resources are developing very rapidly.

In the third chapter we will discuss how to obtain space, equipment, and other resources. For example, we will discuss strategies involved in obtaining funding.

We will describe a strategy that could involve a "nothing succeeds like success" approach in which a researcher might look for justification to seek internal funding, not so much because completing a project could not do without it, but because having received such internal funding might improve one's chances of later obtaining other funding. We will also provide specific examples illustrating how different research methods can make use of the limited resources that may be available at the beginning of a program so as to build a case for asking for more resources to expand a program. For example, we will describe examples of conducting research on teaching methods. This example will illustrate how a research program has to be enlarged by taking small steps first, and then building on them. It will describe in detail some methods that were used successfully to produce data, some of which has already been published and more of which is waiting in the pipeline to be published. This chapter will provide practical advice on choosing research directions including several anecdotes from our experience illustrating both pitfalls and opportunities when choosing a research direction. Here is where we will describe OpenSesame, an open source platform for building experiments to be presented via computer.

In Chapter 4 we will deal with the problem of availability of human subjects. We will describe advantages and disadvantages of methods such as ad hoc recruiting from classes, offering extra credit for research participation, and participation as a course requirement. This chapter will discuss the difficulties and solutions involved in gaining the cooperation of colleagues in order to recruit subjects from their classes. It will discuss similar issues involved in motivating students to participate in research as subjects. For example, there are ethical issues to be dealt with both when recruiting subjects through a subject pool system or when recruiting from classes. Recruiting from classes that the researcher is also teaching in presents special ethical issues. Those problems and their potential solutions will be described. Subject pools will be especially described in detail. This chapter will discuss such problems as how to motivate students to participate without running afoul of the ethical restraint that students are always allowed to withdraw from participation. It will discuss why and how subject pools can be run ethically. It will describe in detail how to emphasize the educational value of participating. This chapter will address the realities of allowing alternative methods of participation to avoid coercion, and engaging the cooperation of fellow faculty in a subject pool system. The chapter will also touch on the use of paper sign up versus web-based sign up methods for a subject pool. Here, we will briefly introduce OpenStax Tutor, an open source initiative that affords ways to build research on instructional methods into classes that are presented on the system.

Chapter 5 will address the issue of using undergraduates as volunteer research assistants. It will present two alternative methods that we call the "exclusive club" and the "open door" method. We will present strategies for advertising, recruiting, managing, and delegating. In this chapter, we provide specific examples of materials, such as flyers, and innovative techniques, such as recording lab meeting minutes as a web page. The chapter will also discuss issues relating to the logistics of taking students to conferences.

Chapter 6 will focus on bureaucratic stumbling blocks. We will distinguish between those problems that probably are to some extent within the control of the researcher versus those that are less so. For those that are more within the researcher's control, we will offer strategies for efficiency, as we did for other issues in previous chapters. For those that are more difficult to control, we will offer ideas to try to foster some beneficial change cumulatively over time, such as by making administrators more aware of the problems.

Chapter Structure and Style

Each of the upcoming chapters will follow a similar format. This consistency will help in clarifying the concepts and understanding the applicability of the material.

Each chapter will begin with specific bullets about what you will either understand or learn in each of the chapters. The chapter will then offer an introduction of the material in the chapter and then will launch into the chapter's narrative. The information will be peppered with specific examples and cases to highlight and illustrate the material. When applicable, specific research will be highlighted and referenced that will offer a scientific grounding for some of the material. Chapters may include figures and tables that will assist in delineating several aspects of the material. Each chapter will conclude with a summary and several suggested readings to further your understanding and information about the topics covered.

One final note about the book's style. Considering that this book is a co-authored project, we use both *I* or *we* as the subject pronoun. In certain places where the discussion is relevant to specific work by one of us, we also use Dr. Ryan or Dr. Milevsky. This is used to enhance the flow of the writing and reading.

Summary

This book will be beneficial to both early career teacher-researchers and those who have been at it for quite a while but are looking for some direction in trying to enhance their research productivity. The book will highlight five specific areas of focus and will offer detailed descriptions of what could be done to enhance and maximize productivity in each of these five areas. The five areas of focus are managing time more effectively, learning how to obtain research space, equipment, and other resources, understanding and navigating the availability of human subjects, utilizing undergraduate research assistants to be part of your research efforts, and finally understanding how to navigate the many bureaucratic stumbling blocks common in university systems.

Combined, an understanding of these five areas will help faculty members increase their research productivity which ultimately will lead them to the eventual goal of achieving academic job satisfaction.

References

Bozeman, B., & Gaughan, M. (2011). Job satisfaction among university faculty: Individual, work, and institutional determinants. *Journal of Higher Education, 82,* 154–186.

Cranny, C. J., Smith, P. C., & Stone, E. F. (1992). *Job satisfaction: How people feel about their jobs and how it affects their performance.* New York, NY: Lexington Books.

Fairweather, J. S. (2005). Beyond the rhetoric: Trends in the relative value of teaching and research in faculty salaries. *Journal of Higher Education, 76,* 401–422.

Gabbidon, S. L., & Higgins, G. H. (2012). The life of an academic: Examining the correlates of job satisfaction among criminology/criminal justice faculty. *American Journal of Criminal Justice, 37,* 669–681.

Hagedorn, L. S. (1996). Wage equity and female faculty job satisfaction: The role of wage differentials in a job satisfaction causal model. *Research in Higher Education, 37,* 569–598.

Hagedorn, L. S. (2000). Conceptualizing faculty job satisfaction: Components, theories, and outcomes. *New Directions for Institutional Research, 105,* 5–20.

Kalleberg, A. (1977). Work values and job rewards: A theory of job satisfaction. *American Sociological Review, 42,* 124–143.

Rockquemore, K. A., & Laszloffy, T. (2008). *The black academic's guide to winning tenure: Without losing your soul.* Boulder, CO: Lynne Reiner.

Rosser, V. J. (2004). Faculty members' intention to leave: A national study on their worklife and satisfaction. *Research in Higher Education, 45,* 285–309.

Sabharwal, M., & Corley, E. A. (2009). Faculty job satisfaction across gender and discipline. *The Social Science Journal, 46,* 539–556.

Seifert, T. A., & Umbach, P. D. (2008). The effects of faculty demographic characteristics and disciplinary context on dimensions of job satisfaction. *Research in Higher Education, 49,* 357–381.

Terpstra, D. E., & Honoree, A. L. (2004). Job satisfaction and pay satisfaction levels of university faculty by discipline type and by geographic region. *Education, 124,* 528–539.

Turner, C. S. V. (2002). Women of color in academe: Living with multiple marginality. *Journal of Higher Education, 73,* 74–93.

Turner, C. S. V., & Myers, S. (2000). *Faculty of color in academe: Bittersweet success.* Needham Heights, MA: Allyn & Bacon.

Watson, R., Storey, D., Wynarczyk, P., Keasey, K., & Short, H. (1996). The relationship between job satisfaction and managerial remuneration in small and medium-sized enterprises: An empirical test of "comparison income" and "equity theory" hypotheses. *Applied Economics, 28,* 567–576.

2
GETTING STARTED AND OVERCOMING TIME CONSTRAINTS

After Reading This Chapter You Will Know How to

- Use the overlapping independent studies strategy
- Increase your efficiency in teaching when using multiple-choice tests
- Be more efficient at grading open-ended responses and papers
- Take advantage of automatic search alerts to facilitate staying current with literature
- Use bibliography software to organize your references
- Use the Open Science Framework to facilitate your entire research workflow

Introduction

One of the most important resources that you need to conduct a research program is your own labor. You are the person with the ideas and the expertise to bring them to fruition. But how can you do that when so much of your time is consumed by your teaching obligations? In this chapter we will present various strategies to increase your efficiency at teaching without sacrificing its quality.

One of the most time consuming tasks involved in research is doing all of the reading that you need to do to stay current with advances in your field. And the reading itself is not the only problem. You read in order to have a knowledge base that you can call on when designing, conducting, and reporting your research. But initially acquiring all that knowledge does you no good if you can't find the information you need when you need it. This chapter will also present several amazing digital resources that can facilitate gathering information, organizing and storing it, and efficiently retrieving it when it is needed.

Starting With What You Have and Building

Starting a research program takes time. It may seem like an overwhelming task at first. It's important to know that it's not just a matter of accomplishing bigger and bigger goals. Seeing it that way can be disheartening. It may seem as if you've put forth tremendous effort at the beginning and only accomplished a small goal. This makes it appear as if larger goals may be unattainable. But what you need to realize is that many of the small goals you achieve provide you with accomplishments on which you will build.

Consider, as an example, building a team of research assistants. At the beginning you may only attract a couple of the more motivated junior or senior students. They, of course, will be leaving in a couple of years, or even next year, or next semester. Then you have to recruit more. But, the word will spread among the students about the benefits of working in your program. Also, you can start taking advantage of club and organization meetings to advertise your program. As word spreads among the students about how beneficial it is to work in your program, you can begin attracting sophomores, and even freshmen. Eventually, you can get to the point where your more veteran research assistants can be recruiting for you. Also, the veteran assistants can help to train the newcomers, thus relieving part of the burden of managing your crew. In other words, instead of being faced with larger and larger tasks as time goes on, the size of your accomplishments will grow naturally because they will be building on previous successes.

Similarly, research projects have a way of extending themselves and spawning more ideas. You may start with an idea for a single experiment. But conducting that first study often leads to new research questions. Of course, at first, with limited manpower, and perhaps limitations on some other resources you need, you can't necessarily tackle more than one project at a time. But, as your research team grows, and as you acquire more resources, you will be able to run more than one project at a time.

The Overlapping Independent Studies Strategy

This may be a good place to introduce the concept of overlapping projects that are in different lines of research, rather than on the same line. I call this the *overlapping independent studies strategy*. At an undergraduate university, when professors pass each other in the hall, the chit-chat often begins with, "How's it going? Are your courses going okay?" That's not what you typically hear at research universities. There, it's, "How's it going? Are you running any subjects?" Producing data by running subjects, although not an end in itself, is at the heart of having a productive research program. We'll have more to say about the nuts and bolts of making a research program productive in future chapters. But, as a start, consider the overlapping independent studies strategy.

According to the overlapping independent studies strategy, you have to be careful about what research questions you tackle, if you tackle more than one at the same time. It may be to your advantage to have two, or even more, research lines that are somewhat independent. The reason for this is because of what it takes to advance research along any one particular line. Typically, you start with a research question, design the study, and then gather the data. But there are more steps that need to be accomplished before you can tackle a new question that may have arisen from that first study. The new research question may not be apparent until you have thoroughly analyzed and digested the data from the first study. By that time, precious weeks or months could have gone by during which you were not running more subjects because the next study had not yet been designed.

But if you had a second line of inquiry that wasn't dependent for its question on the outcome of the first study, then you could already begin to run subjects in that second study. Then, as you are in the process of running the subjects in the second study you could design the follow-up study to the first one. That way, by the time you finished running subjects in the second study, you would be ready to run subjects in the follow-up to the first—without having to wait for the results of the second study, which was not closely related. The result is that, using this strategy, you can be running subjects more of the time than you could if you were trying to always run subjects in the same line of research.

Efficiency in Teaching

Because this book is about how to build a research program even though you are primarily a teacher, it is important to know that building a successful and productive research program does not need to be incompatible with being a good teacher. Undergraduate universities and even community colleges are coming to value more and more the contribution that being an active researcher can make to the quality of your teaching. Nevertheless, to build a research program while being primarily a teacher will require that you teach efficiently, as well as effectively. The two are not incompatible. As a matter of fact, studies examining the factors that are associated with being an expert, versus a novice teacher, have shown that one of the key differences is that the experts are more efficient at using their time (Leinhardt, 1989).

Consider, for example, timely feedback on grades. Grading can be one of the most time consuming activities for a teacher, particularly grading papers. Being able to get through that process efficiently leaves more time for research activities. But, rather than being detrimental to the quality of your teaching, timely feedback is greatly appreciated by your students. It improves their ability to learn by enabling them to focus on their problem areas. If they don't get timely feedback, then they don't know what those areas are in time to focus on them for their next test.

Tests can be in many formats. I'll discuss first some efficiency promoting ideas for multiple-choice tests. Of course, some subjects require more open-ended testing, assigning papers, or both. Grading open-ended responses bears some similarity to grading papers. Therefore, I'll discuss grading papers next, with the assumption that much of what applies to grading a paper will apply to grading open-ended responses.

Multiple-Choice Tests

Multiple-choice tests are ubiquitous in higher education, and for good reason. First, even without the challenges of combining building a research program with a heavy teaching load, teaching benefits from efficiency. Second, multiple-choice tests, when well constructed, can be very useful assessments and have their own unique advantages (Little et al., 2012).

Textbook publishers often include test banks that include more than enough multiple-choice items to construct all the tests you need for a given course. Some publishers provide software that enables you to easily scan through and select questions. Others provide the questions in word processor documents. In either case, the test items can be selects as-is, or modified to suit the teacher's needs. It is wise, however, to carefully read through the questions the first time you select them, as they are sometimes not written as the teacher would want them written, and occasionally contain outright errors that need to be corrected.

A good strategy is to build your courses around the learning objectives that you wish your students to accomplish, and then select questions based on those learning objectives for your tests. It is best to have a sort of master copy of each test. Typically, as you teach any given course, even though you may have taught it many times before, you will cover slightly different material or cover the material in slightly different ways each time you teach it. When it comes time to give a test, you can then go to the master copy and add, delete, or modify questions as needed, according to what you have covered and how you covered it. This provides another example of building on your past accomplishments over time. Modifying a master test to suit your needs may be more time consuming than you would like at first. But with practice and experience it will become easier and faster. Also, with experience teaching the same course repeatedly, you will become better and better at zeroing in on the goals you want your students to accomplish, and have to spend less and less time modifying tests.

Getting to the point where your multiple-choice tests are more similar from administration to administration has the advantage that it enables you to compare performance on the same items on different administrations. Here, a test-item analysis is very useful. You may have a machine scoring device at your disposal that provides such a test-item analysis. If not, it is possible to create a spreadsheet template that grades your tests and does the analysis for you, by simply entering students responses. I created such a template and have used it for many years to give me answer distributions, and item difficulties and discrimination values on my tests (you can download it from https://osf.io/trcwj/). It takes a little longer to enter students' responses into the spreadsheet by hand than it would take to run their answer sheets through a scoring machine. But it doesn't take that much longer. And it has enabled me to use the item analysis that it creates to fine-tune my tests. Furthermore, the item analysis can be used to uncover problem areas for students that need more attention in your teaching.

One final advantage of using such a spreadsheet needs to be mentioned, and that is how easy it is to make changes. You may need to make a change if you discover that you have made a scoring key error, or you may want to change the scoring key to allow more than one answer to be accepted as correct. If you make an error on your scoring key that you don't discover until after you have run all of the students' answer sheets through a scoring machine, you have to correct the key and run them all again. However, with the spreadsheet, all you need to do is correct the key in the spreadsheet, and the formulas in the spreadsheet automatically fix everything else.

Sometimes, the item analysis shows you that students' answers were pretty evenly split between two responses, only one of which you considered the correct response. But I have had the experience that, during the process of giving feedback on a test, a student makes a good argument as to why the other answer that half of the students selected could also be considered correct. Such a situation can be turned to your advantage as one of those valuable "teachable moments" that teachers talk about. In such a situation I have explained to the students that there was a subtle difference that made that second answer incorrect. But, I also acknowledged that because I may not have lived up to my responsibility to make that subtle distinction clear enough either when I initially taught the material or in the way that I wrote the question, the students should not be held accountable for being able to discern the difference. I then thank the student who made the argument, and tell them that I will either try to be clearer in my teaching in the future, or that I will rewrite the question so that it is clearer, or both. Importantly from their perspective, I also tell them that I will go back to my grading spreadsheet, accept both answers as correct this time, and post a correction to their grades. This has the effect of improving my teaching, improving student learning, and buying a great deal of good will on the part of the students, which can be very valuable when it comes time for those teaching evaluations. Because the spreadsheet calculates grades from a set of formulas, changing one formula to allow the two answers to be correct automatically changes everything else so that it is quick and easy to update the students' grades.

I post the item analysis back to a copy of the test that I then use to give the students feedback. My students appreciate the fact that I almost always give them feedback on their tests at the beginning of the class following the class in which the test was given. As part of my standard procedure, before I administer the test, I project a presentation sheet that gives them instructions for their test (Figure 2.1).

You can't leave during the test.

If you need to use the restroom, do so before you start.

Make sure all electronic devices are turned off.

Mark your answers on BOTH the scantron and the test booklet.

Mark both with the answer you intend, so they are the same, however ONLY the scantron
is graded. Therefore, make sure you mark the scantron with the answer you intend.

You may mark up the test booklet as much as you wish.

There is no penalty for guessing, so leave no answers blank.

If you don't understand a question, ASK. If I can clarify it for you without giving away information, I will.

Turn in all materials when you are finished.

FIGURE 2.1 Test instructions.

Notice that those instructions tell them to mark their answers both on their
answer sheets and on their test booklets. This enables me to pass back their test
booklets for their feedback. For test security, I retain their answer sheets and allow
them to see the answer sheet only in my office.

As we go over the test, the item analysis enables me to point out to them questions where they are having particular difficulty, or where there is a particularly
common misconception. It enables the students to check my grading of their tests
against the grade that was posted for them. There are occasionally times when a
student will claim they have discovered a discrepancy. Using this system, such a
discrepancy can be handled very efficiently. They don't need to go into any explanation. I simply tell them to email me, and I'll double check their answer sheet,
my spreadsheet, their test booklet, and the posted grade to find the discrepancy, to
correct it if necessary, and to email them the result. Most often, the discrepancy is
either that they marked their answer sheet differently from the test booklet (the test
instructions warn them that only their answer sheet is graded) or they miscalculated
when they went over their test booklet in the feedback. Occasionally, however,
the mistake is mine. Over time, with practice entering grades into the spreadsheet
from their answer sheets these errors have become much less common. But it still
can happen, once in a great while, that I have entered the wrong answer. But, once
again, because the spreadsheet does all the calculating automatically, it is very easy
to correct. Just by changing the one incorrect entry, all becomes correct again.

Over time, the test item analysis will enable you to have multiple-choice tests
ready to go with little time-consuming preparation. You will be able to prepare,
administer, grade the test, and then give your students feedback more and more
efficiently. At the same time, you will be confident that those tests are providing
you with a valid assessment of what your students know and understand.

When you develop the ability to grade multiple-choice tests quickly, there
arises a slight problem if a student has missed class on the test day. If that student
attends the next class, and you are giving feedback on the test in that next class,
you'll need to ask that student to step out of the class while you go over the test.

Then another student can go and get them so that they can participate in the rest of the class. I usually ask for a volunteer to go and fetch the student who is leaving before they leave. I've learned from experience that it is easy to be anxious to move on after doing the feedback and forget to get that student back. It's a little embarrassing when a student has to remind you to do that!

The problem of students missing a test raises the issue of how to handle such situations efficiently. The need to avoid the problem of having a student have to leave the class while you give feedback on a test, along with your speed at giving that feedback, dictates that if a student misses a class on test day, they must make the test up as soon as possible—preferably the very next day. What about the question of whether the student should be allowed to make up the test? I find that students who miss a test usually immediately send me an apologetic email along with an entreaty to be allowed to make up the test. On the one hand, my syllabus says that if they miss a test, they need to provide documentation of a legitimate reason for missing the test. On the other hand, for more than one reason, I want them to make up the test, and to do so immediately. The first reason, as already mentioned, is to avoid the problem of the student needing to step out of the class on the feedback day. But also, for the sake of the student's success in the course, I don't want them to fall behind. If the student needs to come up with documentation, and then, each time this happens, I have to decide whether the documentation constitutes a legitimate reason, this delays getting the makeup test out of the way. In my experience, students sufficiently dread having to ask for forbearance to make up a test that it deters them from missing tests either deliberately, or totally negligently. More often, there really is an acceptable reason. Sure, there is the occasional sleeping through the alarm in the morning, but who among us has not done that, especially in our younger, formative years. I emphasize to the student how important it is to make up the test as soon as possible, rather than to belabor their reasons for missing the test. You can usually practically hear the relief in their voices when they answer your, "How soon can you make up the test?" with "How about later today or tomorrow?" Yes, there is the risk that some student might take advantage of such leniency. But you can usually catch on to such students. That's why your *syllabus* specifies that you retain the right to require documentation. Because such students are (fortunately) not the norm, you can expect to be able to increase your efficiency by just getting makeup tests out of the way as soon as possible. On balance, I believe that the benefit of the gains in your efficiency, and the benefits to those students who innocently (or at least somewhat innocently) missed a test outweigh the possible costs of students taking advantage.

By way of supporting my argument that you can usually catch on to the student who is truly negligent, I'll pass on this story. One time when I was teaching Experimental Psychology, I had a student who was missing classes. Whenever I would run into him he would always have a good story about why he missed. By the end of the semester he had missed so many classes that he was behind on the final research project for the class. He was so far behind, that he would fail the class unless I allowed him to take an incomplete grade, and finish up the work. I explained to him that in order to qualify for such an accommodation, he would have to sign an agreement with me regarding what he would do to make up the work, and by what time. In addition, because I suspected that his reasons for missing so many classes just might not be legitimate, I told him that in addition to the agreement, he would have to provide me with some acceptable documentation, such as a note from a doctor, verifying the legitimacy of his absences. He had assured me that his absences were legitimate because he claimed that he had been having back trouble, and that his doctor had ordered him not to sit for prolonged periods of time, as in a class.

He brought me a note from the doctor. I read the note and told him that I would get back to him. The reason I told him that I would get back to him was because the note only said that the student was under this doctor's care, but it did not say specifically that the doctor had ordered him to not attend classes. I called the doctor. I explained the situation and asked him if the intention of his note for this student was to provide him with a legitimate excuse for missing classes. There was a momentary silence. I'll never forget what the doctor said next. "Wait 'til I get my hands on that little son-of-a-b-----." I responded, "Thank you, doctor. That's all I needed to know." Needless to say, that student did not get the extension, failed the class, and had to repeat it.

Grading Open-Ended Responses and Papers

As mentioned above, much of what I will have to say about grading papers will also apply to grading other kinds of open-ended responses, such as answers to essay questions. However, grading papers has one particularly aggravating pitfall that I will address first. It is a problem that occurs when students are allowed to revise and resubmit their papers.

If a course ought to be writing intensive, either in the opinion of the professor, or, as often happens now, by fiat from a curriculum committee, then the students ought to have the experience of writing, receiving a review, and rewriting. This is part of preparing them for the world of work for which they may be headed. When we, as professional scholars, receive a review, we understand that the reviewers are usually giving us general advice regarding what they would like to see improved, changed, added, or deleted. We know that they are not rewriting our paper for us. However, do we not still try to discern exactly what they are looking for in order to increase our chances of having the paper accepted on the second submission? I'll admit I do that. How much more can we expect, then, that students, given their inexperience and lower level of scholarly sophistication, will do the same, and even more so? You may have had this experience. It's that student who comes back to you after trying to rewrite an initially terrible paper and demands to know why they didn't get an A on the paper because they "did everything you told them to do." How do you review their paper without rewriting it for them, and yet in a way that is really helpful to them?

It takes practice. As I read a poorly written paper, my first impulse is to try to identify and correct each and every problem as I come to it. That's a bad idea. At least it is a bad idea to try to do that continually throughout the entirety of a poorly written paper. However, some degree of specificity in your corrections is necessary in order to provide the kind of feedback that the student feels is helpful. The problem is that it is not possible to do that for the whole paper. The solution is to get the right balance of specific examples of corrections that can be made and general advice that the student will need to interpret in order to apply it.

When I am at my worst at being too specific I sometimes look back at my written feedback and find that it reads like this: Introduction: First sentence: Grammatical error ...... Second sentence: Incorrect use of "then" for "than"; poor word choice—Studies do not conclude—people conclude—studies show... Third sentence .... and so on. At some point I realize that if I don't change direction I am headed toward writing a review that is longer than the paper! I have to go back and begin the feedback with something like, "There are many examples of sentences that are unclear because of such problems as grammatical errors and choices of words that are poor, completely inappropriate, or simply incorrect. For example… " … " For a very poorly written paper, the examples are followed with, "Such problems continue throughout the paper." With experience, you can give sufficient examples to help the student without falling into the trap of rewriting the paper for the student.

No matter how good you get at the balance, however, some students still do not get it from your feedback. There is still the possibility that they will complain that they "Did everything you told me to do," but still got a poor grade on the final paper. To help even further with this problem, over the years I have developed standard things to tell students right from the start to help forestall the aforementioned problem. I have distilled them into a document entitled "How a paper is judged" (see Appendix) that I put on their Learning Management System (LMS) and go over in class (Figure 2.2).

Of course, it does not eliminate the problem entirely, but it does accomplish a goal that helps you with your research. It minimizes the time you need to spend on the problem.

The other kind of open-ended responses, the grading of which can be time consuming, is essay answers on tests. Making them easier to grade can begin by how the question is written. When you ask for an open-ended response, you have in mind certain things that you are looking for in the answer. How much do you want to tell the student about what you are looking for, and how much do you expect them to know without your leading them? This, like the general advice versus specific examples for papers is a matter of striking a balance.

It is also a matter of thinking ahead. If you are going to ask an open-ended question to which you expect them to know the components that should go into the answer without prompting from the test question, then why not provide that prompting at the time you teach the concept? For example, when teaching about the nature of theories in my Experimental Psychology class,

How a paper is judged

The final grade for a paper is based on how well the paper accomplishes all of its intended goals. Those goals include presenting all of the required information, presenting it in the correct places, and following APA format. But, more importantly, the paper needs to present a clear and coherent story to the reader of what you were trying to accomplish, how you tried to accomplish it, what you found, and what has been learned. Accomplishing those goals requires that the paper's organization, transitions, sentence structure, choice of words, etc. all contribute to the overall clarity and ease of reading of the paper. This is ultimately how the paper is judged.

After you have written a first draft of the paper, you may bring it to me for help. You need to come with questions that are as specific as possible. For example, you might want to know whether a specific statement in your paper requires citing a reference. As long as I know what was in the paper being referred to, and I know what you are saying in your paper, I can give you a yes or no answer. But if you ask me something like, "Is my paper clear enough?" I might have to answer anything from "Yes, it is quite clear" to "It needs some improvement" to "No, I'm having a very hard time understanding it." I probably will not be able to just give you a list of specific things to change to completely solve the problem. Instead, I will have to give you several suggestions for various possible ways to improve the clarity of the paper.

When I suggest changes to a paper I am not rewriting the paper for you. I cannot guarantee that in one sitting it will even be possible for me to make all of the specific suggestions that would need to be made in order make it as good as you want it to be. If the paper needs a lot of work, the most I can do is give you general advice, such as that you must improve your sentence structure, or the overall clarity, etc. and perhaps try to point out a specific example or two of where such changes need to be made. Generalizing the advice from the examples to each place where you need to apply it is up to you. Figuring out the details of how to make the improvements is up to you.

If I give you a specific suggestion to a paper that needs a lot of improvement, it is only a suggestion that might improve the paper. But even following that specific suggestion alone may not make that much of an improvement. The reason that is true is that when I suggest that you change one thing in the paper, making that change might require that you make other changes as well. I cannot tell you what those other changes might be because I will not have read the paper after you made the first suggested change. That is up to you.

The paper is all inter-related. It is even possible that making one of the changes I may have suggested would then make some other change that I suggested a bad idea. You can only see that when you spend the necessary time rewriting the paper. You can bring the rewritten paper to me to get more advice. But you cannot expect that you will keep bringing it back to me over and over until it is as good as you want it to be. If I did that for you, then, again, I would be writing the paper for you, just over many sessions.

So, as you can see, rewriting a paper is not just a matter of getting a list of suggested changes from me and then making those changes. Also, rewriting is not

(Continued)

accomplished by sitting down and doing one rewrite in one sitting. Rather, you need to go through several cycles of rewriting, putting the paper away, coming back to it later when you have had a chance to get away from thinking about it, and rereading and rewriting it again, with all of the above goals in mind.

If you do all that, then you will have a paper that is as good as you can make it, given your particular vocabulary level, your level of ability at precise use of language, and your writing talent. If the quality of the paper you produce is still not as good as you would like it to be, then perhaps you need to work to improve the aforementioned abilities. Doing so is beyond the scope of any single course. It requires that you do things like a lot of serious reading to help you deduce how good writers write. Most of all, becoming a good writer takes a lot of practice.

FIGURE 2.2 How a paper is judged.

I want the students to understand how theories fit into scientific thinking and how they are used. I want them to learn how scientists view theories as something different from what the non-scientist typically thinks. I want them to know the characteristics of a better theory versus one that is not as good. In my teaching, I emphasize that understanding the nature of a theory requires understanding all of those components. Then, when I write an essay question probing their knowledge of the nature of theories, I don't mind asking the question as a series of components: "What is a theory, according to a scientist, as opposed to according to a non-scientist? What would be an example of a misconception about how theories are used in science? What makes a theory a good theory?"

As a different example, when I teach about the problems caused by the various different kinds of carryover effects in a within subjects design and how they can be remedied, I am also teaching several different components that go into a full understanding of the concept. But I tell the students that the carryover effects differ in their complexity, and the remedies differ in their complexity in a corresponding way. I point out that I start with the simplest problem, which has the simplest remedy, and I work to the most complex problem, which has the most complex remedy. I advise them that it is to their advantage to organize their knowledge of this topic in order from the simplest to the most complex. Then, when I write an essay question probing their knowledge of this topic, I simply ask "What are the various types of carryover effects, and how can they be remedied?" In this case, I leave it to the students to remember the useful organizational tool to help them answer the question.

Of course, one could just as easily ask the question about theories with no reference to the components that should go into the answer, and ask the question about carryover affects with a reference to a good organization for the answer. The point is that by using this approach it is possible to strike a good balance regarding how much to expect from your students when answering open-ended questions and also to put yourself in a good position to be able to grade their answers efficiently. You can choose to provide as little or as much guidance regarding the components of a good answer as you choose. But you can always feel you are grading in a fair way by grading, at least in part, according to how many of the necessary components the student included in their answer.

You may at certain times feel, as I sometimes do, unsure about just how much to expect from your students in an essay answer. In that case, you can always use the strategy of using two passes through their answers. That is, you can go through their answers in the first pass to see what components the students have actually included. Make a list. You may find that only the strongest students have included certain components that you know from experience are the most difficult for your students to learn. For example, I find that students have a lot of difficulty catching on to the idea that scientists do not consider theories to be merely speculations that need to be "proven" correct, in which case they then become a "fact." Students have tremendous difficulty understanding that a theory's being, at least in principle, always tentative implies that scientists do not even have the intention to prove that their theory is correct, and that scientists therefore do not evaluate theories on correctness per se, but rather, on other criteria. If no student expresses the most difficult idea in their answers, you may decide to give full credit even for an answer that does not include that most difficult idea. Whatever you decide, it can be based on the list of components that do, or do not, appear in the student's answers. The point is, by using this approach, you can speed up your grading process by not agonizing over what grades to give the first answers you see without knowing what you may or may not see in the others. And at the same time, you can feel that you used your analysis of how well the students have learned the material to guide your grading to be fair, and properly balanced between stringency and leniency.

The above discussion of grading essay answers naturally leads to the question of whether to use a rubric, whether in grading essay answers or papers. In my opinion, I do see value in using a rubric, although I question whether the rubric needs to be written out in advance. The same approach that I described above for grading essay answers can be applied to grading papers as well. But should there be a rubric spelled out in advance as to what should be in the paper? Should that rubric be provided to the students?

From the discussion of how a paper is judged, it should be apparent that providing a rubric in advance runs the same risks as reviewing a paper that is to be revised. That is, how do you avoid the risk that a student will write a very poor paper, yet still be able to argue that they "did everything they were told to do" by the rubric. The only way around this is that the rubric has to include some percentage of the grade for something like "clarity of expression," or "ease of readability." In my experience, in order for following the rubric to lead to what any professor would consider appropriately stringent grading, that percentage has to be pretty high. In other words, the rubric needs to leave enough flexibility for the professors to apply their own judgment to a sufficient extent.

The way I have always handled this issue is to spend several class periods teaching what the goals of each section of an empirical paper should be. Then, I also provide examples of how those goals were met by analyzing a published paper or two. In an Experimental Psychology class, in which one has students do their own research projects, examples can come from those sources as well. I also provide students with examples of poorly written papers and a corrected version of such a paper (Figure 2.3).

Poorly written paper

People learn through examples, these examples can be directly applied in testing when the questions are very similar or exact to the prior learned example (Anderson, Fincham, & Douglass, 1997). Testing can further be enhanced through the use of shuffling or interleaving the examples. That is to say, studying one example following by several examples of the same concept leads to *poorer* performance than several examples of different and interleaved concepts. Rohrer and Taylor (2007) supported this hypothesis by shuffling, or interleaving, examples of geometrical problems. By interleaving the geometry problems (versus blocking) Rohrer and Taylor facilitated *better* with performance. Likewise, Kornell and Bjork (2008) revealed that blocking the examples of painting styles lead to *poorer* performance on style recall and that, interleaving examples led to *better* performance.

Corrected version

Studying examples is an important way for people to learn. For instance, LeFevre and Dixon (1986) showed that people prefer to learn from examples rather than from instructions. Furthermore, they can apply what they learned from training examples to similar test examples (Anderson, Fincham, & Douglass, 1997). However, does the acquisition and retention of knowledge gained from examples depend on how they are presented? For example, in teaching students to learn several different concepts, teachers could present examples in *blocks*, that is, several examples of one concept, followed by several examples of another. But they could also present them *interleaved*, that is, the examples of the different concepts could be mixed so that each example of a particular concept was always followed by an example of a different concept. Rohrer and Taylor (2007) showed that people learned to solve geometrical problems better if they were trained with interleaved rather than blocked examples. However, their study showed a benefit of interleaving only for learning in geometry. Kornell and Bjork (2008) questioned whether the benefit of interleaving would extend to learning to categorize painting styles. They hypothesized that for that task people might benefit from being able to compare several examples of the same style presented one right after the other. Thus, they hypothesized that in this case blocking might be superior to interleaving. However, they found that interleaving was superior in this case as well.

FIGURE 2.3 A poorly written paper and a corrected version.

When we go through that example, I let them read the poorly written paper and ask them if they understood what the writer meant. I admit there is something therapeutic about giving them a taste of how painful that process is. Then, when we examine the better written version, I do not dissect it as in showing them "this is what you need to change to get a good grade." Instead, I just let them read the more clearly written paper and let them experience the relief one feels when reading something that is easy to understand after reading a garbled version first. I tell them that this is done in order to help them to understand what I mean by "The overall most important goal of your writing is its clarity and ease of readability." This comes in very handy when it comes time for them to understand why they got the grade they got on the paper.

I let my instruction to them of what the goals are for each section of an empirical paper and the other exercises I described above stand in place of giving them a written rubric for writing their papers. I even tell them that if they want to have a rubric in front of them as they write, then they should take good notes in the class where we go over the goals and use that as their rubric if they wish. But I also remind them that the ultimate goal is that their writing should be so clear that it is easy to read and understand. I even give them the standard advice to "Try reading it to your grandmother. If you can explain it clearly to her, you have probably explained it as clearly as you need to."

Using Conferences to Pre-grade Papers

One other tactic for increasing the efficiency of grading papers deserves special mention. That tactic is to schedule individual conferences with students to answer their questions and to give them advice on writing their papers. I typically set up my syllabus for my Experimental Psychology course, which is designated as a writing intensive course, so that there are several class periods devoted to those conferences.

That, of course, raises the question of whether it is acceptable to use class time for that purpose. I have found that I have never had to defend that tactic to the chair of my department, although there is no guarantee that your experience will be the same. Admittedly, the first time I did it, I went ahead without asking anyone, on the assumption that, as they say, it may be easier to get forgiveness than permission. Perhaps one reason why it was easily accepted was that, at least the first time I did it, the schedule for the conferences took up all the class time of about three classes, plus more time. Thus, there was no question that I was working, in effect, overtime for the benefit of my students, rather than trying to weasel out of some of my responsibilities.

I have continued to use this approach over the years in several variations and have never had it called into question. Even the fact that it results in each student being free from attending some class time while other students are in their conferences has not been a problem. This is because in the classes where I have used this approach the students also are required to do projects in which they are required to spend a good amount of out of class time gathering data. So it all balances out.

Of course, whether you schedule conferences in such a way that you put in extra teaching time, or fit all of them into the regular class time is up to you. It will partly depend on how many students are in the class and how much time you allot for each conference. I have, at times, scheduled as much as 30 minutes for each conference. This was done when I had fewer students. Nevertheless, this takes more than the regular class time, but it provides ample time to discuss the student's writing. I have also scheduled as little as 15 minutes per student. I did that when I had more students. I was not able to do that until I had used the tactic several times, and had built up experience at reading the paper and giving the advice more efficiently than when I did it for the first time. Also, another thing I had learned from experience was to give myself frequent breaks. Doing those conferences is very demanding work, and you need a chance to catch your breath and clear your head after doing a few of them. When scheduling 15-minute sessions, I schedule 3 for any given hour and then there's a 15-minute break. That allows me to run a little over with some students (hopefully not so much that you use up too much of your break time) and still be able to start the next hour on time.

Another question that arises is how to go about scheduling the students for the times. One strategy is to make up a signup sheet and let the students pick their own times. But I have found that this strategy does not work well. How do you get around the problem of the unfairness of the first students who get the sheet picking the most desirable times? A possibility is to not hand out the sheet in class. Rather, you can post it on your office door and announce in class that students are to sign up. Then, perhaps, you can assume that the most diligent students sign up first, and therefore, if they get the best times, they deserve it. But it could be that some students arrive to sign up later not because they are less diligent, but for some other reason, such as they had another class right after the one in which you announced the availability of the signup sheet. Another problem can occur if you make the signup sheet so that it has more time slots than you have students, which you may do in order to allow some flexibility. I have found that the way the students use that "flexibility" is to sign up as late as possible on the schedule. Thus, you may end up with unused time at the beginning of the schedule, and a packed schedule at the end, thus eliminating the flexibility that you desired to have.

To avoid all of the problems above, I eventually, again, with experience, went to the system of assigning the times myself. I generate a column of random numbers (statistical or spreadsheet programs can do this for you) and put that column next to my column of students' names in my grading spreadsheet. Then, I use the spreadsheets function to sort on the random numbers, including the students' names in the sort. Then I can copy that randomly sorted list of students' names to a column next to a column with the conference times, print it out, and, there you have it. Make copies to hand out to the students and tell them that these are their conference times. A word of warning: If you have more than one section, be sure to randomize within sections so that you don't sched-ule students in one section for a conference in the other section's class time (as I did the first time I tried this).

This tactic works well if you have scheduled all of their conference times within the class time. If some of the conference times are out of class time, then you run the risk that you've scheduled a student at a time that they cannot come. In such a case, however, as long as the problem does not occur for too many stu-dents, it may be as simple as asking for a volunteer to switch times. If you need to schedule a relatively large number of conferences out of class time, then you may be able to use a hybrid approach in which you determine in advance which students are available only during class time, and which ones are available during an out of class time, and then randomize them within those times.

The whole reason for using this approach is to increase your efficiency without sacrificing the quality of your teaching. During the conferences you provide an opportunity for the student to ask you, one on one, any questions they have about how to write the paper. In order for that to be most helpful for them, it is impor-tant that they know in advance that they are to bring to the conference as finished and polished a draft as they can. I always tell my students not to bring me what they would consider a first draft of the paper. Rather, I tell them that I expect to see a finished, polished product. I expect them to have written and rewritten the paper before they even bring it to me. They will not even know what problems they are having or what questions to ask if they don't do that. During the confer-ence, I evaluate and critique the paper as described at the beginning of this section where I describe how to grade open-ended responses and papers. Of course, in this case I'm doing it verbally and, as it were, on the fly.

For a paper that is poorly written, it takes some practice to develop the ability to give an honest critique while being considerate of the student's feelings. After reading a completely unintelligible sentence to myself, I'll just honestly tell the student, "I don't know what you mean here." Then I'll ask them to read the sen-tence out loud to me. Usually, they immediately realize that the problem is that they themself didn't know what they meant to say. Many times I have asked such a student to forget about writing a paper for a moment, and to just, first, think about what they meant, and then say it to me out loud in their own words. I'll emphasize that they should try to express their thought in a complete, grammati-cal sentence, but one that is as short and as simple as possible, and uses vocabu-lary that they are familiar with—no fancy jargon. Sometimes it takes them more than one try (a very useful example of the importance of rewriting in itself), but they usually end up giving me a perfectly good, meaningful, and understandable sentence. I often ask them to repeat it. Then I ask them, "Why didn't you just write that?" It makes them begin to realize what the mental process of organiz-ing their thoughts before they try to write them down is all about. Often they seem surprised. "Oh. Is that what I'm supposed to do?" Yes. That's what you're supposed to do.

Importantly, during such a conference I encourage, even require, the student to take notes. I often have them bring two hard copies of the paper—one for them to annotate, and one for me. However, here is where the real efficiency producing part comes in. I also have a note pad on which I make some notes for my eyes only. Those notes serve as a reference for me to use later in which I am essentially pre-grading the paper. That is, I'm annotating how I would have graded the paper had the conference version been the final version. I have learned that in those notes I need to make reference to the overall impression that I had of that particular paper that I'm going to need to remind myself of when I do grade the final paper. Thus, when I receive the revised version of the paper to grade, I don't have to take the time to read it as if I were reading it for the first time. I have already done that in the conference. By looking at my notes from the conference, I can quickly skim through the final paper and just note by checking a sampling of the writing whether its clarity was improved. I have learned from experience using this approach that students who bring a very poorly written paper to the conference usually only improve a little, if at all, in terms of the clarity of their writing. The grade that you would have given the paper if you had graded the conference version usually is not that different from the grade you give the actual final paper. And, not to worry, if a paper is improved substantially, then by referring to the conference notes, and even just skimming the final version, that improvement will be apparent, and your final grade can very fairly reflect that improvement. This approach can accomplish the goal of making the process of grading papers much more efficient, while maintaining both the intellectual integrity and the fairness of the grades. From the students' point of view, this approach is seen as one of the most valuable things that you do in the course. I know that is true from the open-ended comments I have received in many student evaluations.

The end result of the approaches described above has been that I have increased my efficiency at some of the most demanding and time consuming tasks involved in teaching, and I have done so in a way that not only does not hurt my students' learning, but even helps it. And, most importantly from my perspective, it has increased the time and energy that I have left to apply to my research program.

Digital Resources to Increase Efficiency in Designing and Conducting Research

The process of finding a good research question, designing a study, carrying out that study, and getting the findings published is very labor intensive. It starts with the challenge of keeping up with the current literature. You do not want the reviewers of your manuscript complaining (as has happened to me) that you are not familiar enough with the latest findings in the field. Then there are the tasks of creating stimulus materials, tests, analysis plans, and scripts for your experimenters to follow as they run your procedure. When the data starts pouring in, there is the task of scoring, coding, and entering the raw data. Then the raw data has to be examined, cleaned up, and put into the formats required for whatever computer program you are going to use to analyze it. When you have the results, you then have to write them up for journal submission. And by the time you have gotten from the beginning of the process (familiarizing yourself with the latest literature) to the point of writing it up, there may be new findings in the literature that you need to address.

In this section, we will present several online digital resources that can facilitate the labor intensive tasks involved in conducting research. They will be organized according to the tasks listed above. That is, there are resources to help with staying current with the literature, facilitating the workflow involved in everything from creating stimulus materials to managing data, and new and improved methods for disseminating the results of your research. We will also briefly introduce open source software for facilitating collecting data, which will be discussed in more detail in future chapters.

It is very important to keep in mind that Internet resources are changing, developing, and improving all the time. The resources that we present here are a snapshot of what is available at the time of this writing. You can be sure that when you read this, some of the resources will have developed beyond what is described here, there will be new ones, and it is possible that some could be gone. But by becoming familiar with the state of the art at this time you will be in a better position to delve into them at whatever time you read this. We will try both to describe the details of some of the resources, which may change, but which will give you a basis for developing a better understanding of these types of resources, and also to describe them in some general ways that will facilitate your looking for and making use of whatever new things may come along.

Staying Current with the Literature

Research builds on previous research. We need to know what has been uncovered before in order to generate good new research questions. I teach my students that a good research question is one that is both on the cutting edge and doable with the resources you have available. That can be a hard combination to find. One can always generate research ideas from some armchair theorizing. For example, I'd love to examine which parts of the brain are differentially activated when people think about taking revenge for a perceived injustice by violent means versus getting the "best" revenge by just living well. What a fascinating question (well, at least to me it's fascinating). The problem is I don't have any brain imaging facilities. And if I did, I'm not trained in how to use them.

So, instead, how about if I present a written scenario to subjects in which they are instructed to imagine having been the victim of some terrible injustice, and then I … what? Measure their heart rate? Give them a problem solving task requiring focusing attention? Surely I can come up with an idea for something that I can measure that might be affected by my manipulation, all of which are doable within the scope of the means that I have available. But who would be interested in whatever I find? How is it related to the current literature that is already out there? I might go to all the labor of designing, running, analyzing, and writing up my experiment, only to receive a review that dismisses my work as "not well situated within the current body of literature."

Automatic Search Alerts

So, one needs to know what is already out there in that "body of literature." And it's huge. And it's growing. It's growing quite rapidly. And at an ever increasing rate! How is one to keep up? Fortunately, modern digital databases are searchable by keywords. You can also search by a number of other criteria, such as author, title, year, etc. But given the enormity of the task, even using such search facilities eats up a lot of time. Even more fortunately, there are now facilities for doing *automatic search alerts.*

If you Google search on the term *automatic search alerts,* you will find that there are many such facilities. At the top of the results list will probably be Google's automatic search alerts. Google's search alert facility is easy to use, and has many helpful features. However, as I always warn my students, searching on Google is not the same thing as searching a database of peer reviewed literature, such as PsychINFO.

As another example to illustrate just how advanced this digital technology has become, the National Center for Biotechnology Information (NCBI) has its own automatic search facility. In the case of a biotechnology researcher this kind of facility appears to be critically needed, given that the NCBI has databases ranging from "Assembly" and "Bioproject" through "Epigenomics" and "Homologene," all the way to "Taxonomy" and "Unigene"—a list of 43 different databases in all. Seeing that makes me glad I'm only a humble psychological science researcher, not a biologist. I only point this out in order to emphasize that documented knowledge is so huge now that all researchers need technology to facilitate searching through it.

The automatic search facility that I use is the Web of Science. I became familiar with it because that is the product to which my university has an institutional subscription. If you need to know what products are available to you through your university, your best bet is to ask a reference librarian. Using the Web of Science automatic search alerts one can specify the search terms to use, and what fields to search (e.g., author, topic, etc.). You can give that particular search a brief name that is meaningful to you, as you may want to set up several searches. Then you can specify the email to which to send any results of the search, how much or how little information you want to receive, in what format you wish to receive it, and how often you want the search to be executed.

I have had the same set of several searches running for several years now. Here is an example of how useful I have found them. Over the seven semesters starting from the fall semester of 2008 through the fall semester of 2011 I ran a series of experiments examining the application in my Statistics classrooms of a cognitive principle of learning that had previously been shown to improve learning in the laboratory. Briefly, it had previously been shown that studying some worked examples, instead of just solving problems, improved learning concepts in mathematics (Sweller & Cooper, 1985). Also, when students are trying to learn to distinguish between several categories by studying examples illustrating those categories, it is better to present the examples by interleaving the different types, rather than presenting blocks of all the same type (Rohrer & Taylor, 2007; Taylor & Rohrer, 2010). And, finally, it had previously been shown that interleaving examples improved learning of not only perceptual categories, but also of conceptual ones (Kornell & Bjork, 2008).

In my experiments I had been trying to apply those findings to improve my Statistics students' learning of which statistical procedure was appropriate for analyzing the data from various different research designs. However, I was not finding convincing evidence of the usefulness of interleaving examples for this classroom application. Meanwhile, I had several automatic searches set up to alert me of any new papers about applying cognitive principles to classroom practice. In 2012, one of those searches turned up a paper by Koedinger, Corbett, and Perfetti (2012). In that paper, the authors introduce what they call the Knowledge-Learning-Instruction framework (KLI). They broke down learning into different types based on cognitive principles. They then broke down the literature on the various instructional methods that have been shown to be effective for the different types of learning. The upshot of that breakdown was that I should not have expected interleaving of examples to be an effective teaching tool to improve learning for the type of material I was trying to teach my Statistics students. On the other hand, the previous research suggests that different teaching tools, such as spacing of practice, practicing retrieval, or prompting the students to explain the examples, might be helpful for learning this particular type of material. Needless to say, the next experiments in the series that I worked on developing examined the effects of those teaching tools. At this writing, the results of those experiments are just coming in. But now, thanks to the search alert that led me to the Koedinger et al. (2012) paper I have the perfect way to "situate my research well within the current body of literature."

If you can keep up with finding papers that are relevant to your research, the next thing you have to do is file them somewhere where you will be able to find them when you need them. Nowadays we store papers as electronic files rather than as paper files (or at least you should, for reasons explained below). However, that in itself does not solve the problem. An electronic filing system still requires that you decide on an organizational structure that makes sense to you, so that you will be able to remember it. The important point is that it has to not just make sense to you now, but rather, it has to continue to make sense to you at a future time when you need to go looking for a particular paper. Coming up with such a sensible system in advance is not so easy. When you start out you may have in mind a certain way to organize your research projects, and so it makes sense to you to organize the literature relevant to those projects in the same hierarchical fashion. But down the road you may discard some projects, start new ones, and rearrange some of them.

Fortunately, electronic copies are a lot easier to arrange and rearrange than hard copies. That's why you should use electronic copies of your literature, only making a hard copy for those times when you know you'll have an opportunity to read a paper that you need to read, but you also know that it will be more convenient to read from a hard copy than an electronic one. It would even be possible to have more than one way to organize your papers, if that would be helpful. For example, you might want to organize them by research questions. But you might also have several different research projects, some of which cite the same paper. Therefore, you might want to also organize them by research projects. You might even want to also use some of those papers in some courses that you teach. And so, it might be also useful to have yet a third organizational structure by course, or topics within courses.

One way to have multiple hierarchical organizational structures would be to create multiple hierarchical folder structures on your computer (two problems that arise, that will be dealt with below, are how to maintain backup copies and how to have easy access to your files even if you are not in your office). You could put copies of your papers in each of those structures. But that might mean that you have to keep multiple copies of the same paper. That uses up storage space, and, if you annotate a copy, the annotations are only in that copy. It might be the case that you want different copies with their own annotations relevant to a particular project or class. If so, then multiple copies are okay. But, there might also be times when you want to make notations that you would want to appear in more than one copy. If the latter is the case, then one solution would be have one folder in which you have all of your papers listed alphabetically as you would in a reference list, and then, in the folders, create links to the original copy. But that still does not solve several other problems. Wouldn't it be nice if there were some kind of software that enabled you to do the kind of linking within multiple folder structures, and maybe solve some of those other problems as well?

Bibliography Software

I did a Google search on the term "bibliography software" and several items came up. At the top of the list was Zotero.org. All the rest were .coms. I have used Zotero for several years now. It is open source. For many years I have preferred to use open source software for any application that I can, both for philosophical reasons, and because, in my opinion, open source software is superior to its proprietary counterparts.

Zotero is an add-on to both your Internet browser and your word processor. It can be used with both of the major proprietary operating systems, and the proprietary Internet browsers and word processors that are usually used with them. It can also be used with open source browsers and word processors, either on proprietary operating systems or on an open source operating system, such as one of the many flavors of Linux OS's.

Here is how it works with your browser. First, I have found it easy to install from the Zotero.org website. Along with installing the software, you create an account on the Zotero website. Once installed on your browser, here is what it does. First, you search for a source in the literature, either by using a database such as PsychINFO, or by doing a general Internet search. When you find a source, or a group of them, an icon appears in the URL box of your browser. Click on that icon and a window appears in which you will see the source, or a list of the sources if there are several, along with check boxes. Check the ones you want to add to your literature library, click on OK, and Zotero downloads that item to your Zotero library, along with all of the information you would need for your citation and your reference list. This library is on the hard drive of the computer on which you are working at the time, but it also syncs to the Zotero website.

If there is a .pdf of the full text, Zotero will download that and attach it to the item in your library as well. Your browser will also have an icon for you to click to go to that library. The library comes up either as a half page at the bottom of your browser window, or you can make it a full page on a new tab in your browser. Either way, you will see a navigation pane on the left, in which you can create, organize, or delete folders in which you can place the items in your library. In the center pane is a list of the items either in your whole library, or in a folder, if you click on one in the navigation pane. On the right is another pane that shows you the citation and reference information that has been downloaded. The library is automatically synced with a Zotero account that you create on their website. If you install Zotero on another computer and associate it with that account, it will automatically sync with that computer as well. Thus, you can install Zotero on your office and home computer and have access to all of the same literature through Zotero. Also, if you are, let's say, away at a conference, and you are using some other computer than your own which does not have Zotero added to the web browser, you can still go to your account on the Internet and access your library that way.

The Zotero library maintains one master copy of each of your sources, but you can drag and drop to any folder in any hierarchical structure you create, and the item will appear there as well. It is actually a link to the master copy, not a whole new copy. However, if you wish to make different annotations to the source for different purposes (your research, or your teaching, for instance) that is easy to do. So, Zotero solves the problem of having multiple ways of organizing your papers so that you can always find them easily. It solves the problem of being able to access your library from anywhere, and it does both of those things without actually using up any more storage space than necessary. And it does so much more.

As explained above, Zotero is an add-on to your word processor, as well as your browser. When you add Zotero to your word processor, several icons appear at the top of the window. Here is how they work. Suppose you are working on a paper and as you are typing along you realize that a claim you just made requires a citation. You remember that you have read a paper that you need to cite. Click on the "insert citation" icon. A box appears that enables you to select the citation and reference format (I would be selecting "APA sixth edition"). Then you can select how you want to search through your library (I chose a method that lets me see the folder structure I have created because that's the easiest way for me to find the paper). You can then find the paper you want, click on it, and the citation will be put into your document. At the end of writing the paper (or anytime you wish, actually) you can put your cursor where you want the reference list to appear, click on another icon, and Zotero inserts the entire reference list, formatted as you have selected. There are also ways to insert multiple citations all at the same time, edit citations, and edit the reference list. But wait, there's more.

This is a feature of Zotero that makes me appreciate it the most. Suppose that when you realize you need to cite a source for something you have said in your paper, you only have a vague memory of what that source might be. You know that you read a paper (maybe years before) that was relevant to this issue. But you can't remember the authors' names or the title of the paper. How are you going to find that paper? I had an experience once, before I discovered Zotero, in which I could really have used it. I was writing a paper in which I wished to assert that a problem with my study could have been the level of motivation of the subjects. I remembered that I had read a paper in which the authors had failed to replicate a previous result on one attempt, but succeeded on another attempt (McKoon & Ratcliff, 1992). They noted, in a footnote, that in the failed attempt they had used subjects who were participating in a Winter and Spring quarter (and thus had already participated in some of the authors' previous reaction time experiments), and that they had used an experimenter who was an undergraduate work-study student who was around the same age as the subjects. On the other hand, when they succeeded, they had used subjects who were mostly freshmen, participating in the fall semester (and therefore participating in their first experiment) and that the experimenter was a recent graduate and therefore older than the subjects. They attributed the difference between the successes of the two attempts to the difference in the motivation of the subjects. But when I remembered that paper, all I remembered was that I had noticed the authors' explanation was the same as in a similar problem that I had encountered when running my first subjects as a grad student. I couldn't remember the authors' names. I certainly did not remember the title because that reference was not about anything related to what I was writing about. As a result, I spent a lot of time hunting until I had finally dug up that reference. Since that time, I have had occasion to refer to the issue of the effects of subjects' motivation on research in my Experimental Psychology class. Each time I needed that reference, I remembered that there was such a reference, but every time I had to go looking for it I started out with the same feeling of frustration that "I know I've hunted for the paper several times before, but I'll be darned if I can remember where I eventually found it." As a matter of fact, as I am writing this, I have just finished going through the same laborious search. This time, however, I made sure that once I found a hard copy of the paper (there was no point in doing an electronic search because what I was looking for was buried in a footnote and would have been very unlikely to come up), I then looked it up in PsychINFO, and put it in my library.

Importantly, Zotero has a feature that will make that the last time I ever have to go through that frustrating search. In Zotero, you can make your own notes about whatever you wish about the reference. Then, those notes are searchable electronically. For the McKoon and Ratcliff (1992) paper, I made a note with the information in the preceding paragraph about the effects of unmotivated versus motivated subjects. Every time I think about that paper, the words "semester" and "unmotivated" come to mind as related to the purpose for which I would want to cite that paper. As I write this, just a moment ago, after making the note in Zotero, I tried to see how quickly I could find the paper in Zotero. I began typing "unmotivated" in the search box, and before I even finished typing the word, that paper popped up. If only I had had Zotero earlier, how much time I could have saved.

The above example of bibliography software is just one example of the kinds of digital and Internet resources that can increase your efficiency in designing and conducting research. However, there is more to increasing that efficiency than just automatic search alerts and bibliography software to help you stay current with the literature. Using the previous literature to help inform your research is just the beginning of a larger process. After you have found a good research question and have come up with an idea for a good design to answer it, there may still be such processes as creating stimulus materials, and writing a script to document your procedures. As you collect data, there may be raw data to be managed and output of analyses and drafts of papers to be kept organized.

A problem that can cause serious delays for any researcher, although especially for a researcher who is trying to collaborate with a colleague (and this might be especially likely for a researcher working at a teaching university) is that the various files that we use are often located in a variety of different locations. Consider a situation in which a researcher needs some materials, or some raw data, or some analysis output from a colleague. The colleague might have to answer the request with something like, "Gee, that stuff is from several years ago. One of my students worked on that and she probably has the files you need. I'll check with her. But, you know, she has since then received her degree and moved on. I'll have to find out where she is and see if I can contact her. I hope she still has that old laptop she was using, or has backed up the files. Let me get back to you." It could end up being quite a nightmare trying to track down the files you need.

There was a not-for-profit organization, the Center for Open Science (COS), founded in 2013 that has developed an invaluable tool to help solve the problem described above. I encourage you, if you are not already familiar with this organization, to visit its website at https://cos.io (they are the masters of short URLs). Early in its development it recognized the need for a tool to help solve the potential nightmare problem described above. The result was the Open Science Framework (OSF). Anyone can go to its website at https://osf.io and create an account. It is open source and free (although note that on the COS home page there is a link to make a donation—certainly a worthy cause).

The OSF is one of the newest of the Internet-based digital resources presented in this book. Although in the beginning of this section on digital resources I mentioned that such resources are a moving target, my guess is that the OSF will be around for a long time. You can, of course, go to its website and learn about it by browsing its website. You can also join the OSF Google group and get on its email list. To join the OSF Google group and get on its email list, just do a Google search on "OSF Google Group," and click on "Open Science Framework—Google Groups." That will bring you to the public page of the group, which you can read, but not post to unless you are a member. At the top of the public page there should be a "Join" button. Here, I will summarize some of the most important features of the OSF.

The OSF has features that facilitate the entire research workflow process. It can be used to great advantage by experienced researchers and students. Among the many things it does, the OSF serves as a cloud storage service for all of your electronic documents. It allows you to easily upload and download files. It automatically creates and displays a record of all activities. When you upload a new version of a file (as you would do in the process of developing such things as stimulus materials or a procedure script) it automatically updates the file to the new version, but also saves the old version. You can easily click on a file and see all of the previous versions, along with the dates and times they were uploaded, as well as who uploaded them.

Your OSF account is organized into "Projects." A project can be anything that you want it to be. Of course, most commonly it will be a particular research project. But it could also be a class that you teach. It could be a research group. It could be either a group of colleagues collaborating together, or your group of volunteer undergraduate research assistants. Or it could be a publication you are working on (this book, at this writing, is one of my projects on the OSF).

Each project can be either private or public. For example, once you have completed a research project, if you wish to make all of your materials, raw data, analysis scripts, and output openly available to other scientists, you can do so, using the OSF. Each project and sub-component of the project can have its own URL. If a colleague emails you and asks if they could use some materials from one of your experiments in their new project, the nightmare scenario described above can be replaced with, "Sure. Go to osf.io/wvnyc and have at it. Good luck. Keep me informed." (That URL, by the way, is for my public profile on the OSF, which you are welcome to visit.)

Each project can have only you as the contributor, or, there can be multiple contributors. Each contributor can have administrator privileges, or read-write privileges, or just read privileges. The contributors have to have an account on the OSF, but it is easy for anyone to create one. On your account, you would be, by default, the administrator of any project. As the administrator you can add or delete contributors and set their privileges. This can all be done with a private project. Thus, you can control who has access to what on your project. For example, I have a project entitled "Ryan Lab Group—Applying Cognitive Methods in Education (ACME)". As undergraduates volunteer to work on research with me, I have them create an OSF account, and I add them to that project as contributors with read-write privileges.

Each project can have components. This creates a hierarchical structure. The components are just like projects except they are associated with a project as their parent in the hierarchy. You can tell that this website was designed and built by people who are thoroughly familiar with information science because its organization all makes so much intuitive sense that it is easy to learn. The sensible character starts with the hierarchical organization. Then, if you need to carry out any function on any component (for example, let's say you decide that you need to rename a file), you just click on the component and above it appears a set of buttons to carry out the functions that would be logically associated with that component. For example, if you click on a document, the document appears in a new window. Above the window are buttons to "Download" or "Delete." There is also a "Check out" button. That button allows you to prevent any other contributors from editing, deleting, or uploading new versions of the file while you have it checked out. Thus, you can edit the file without worrying about conflicting copies appearing because another contributor unwittingly edited it at the same time that you did. Then when you are done, you can check the file back in.

Among the many other features of the OSF are, for example, that the components can have categories, such as "Methods and Material" or "Data," which can be used to help with organization, or they can just be "Other." Your files on your OSF account can be associated with other cloud-based services that you might already use, such as Dropbox or GitHub. There are too many other features of the OSF to mention them all here. As mentioned above, you can create your own account and examine the site for yourself to see the other features. I'll just say here that I have found the OSF to be an amazingly valuable tool to help me speed up my research work and keep it organized. And there is one more feature that I cannot leave unmentioned, and that is the ability to pre-register a project.

I was taught, as you probably were, that the research process goes something like this: First you search the literature to find and refine a good research question.

Then you develop a good method for answering your question. If you are using human or non-human animal subjects, you get IRB approval. Then you collect your data. You analyze the data to see if your hypothesis was supported. If not, and even if so, you further delve into your data for other valuable findings. Then you write up your results and begin submitting them for publication. As researchers with integrity, we only make claims that can be supported by our evidence. But in addition to using our data to inform our original hypothesis, we want to increase the value of our data by doing some exploration of it. And the process I have just described leaves open the possibility of blurring the line between data exploration and slipping into capitalizing on chance. Furthermore, the tremendous pressures on researchers, especially those who are new to the field, to publish in order to advance their careers can lead to falling into questionable practices both in psychology (Simmons, Nelson, & Simonsohn, 2011) as well as in research generally (Ioannidis, 2005). We were also taught that the process of attempting to replicate results is the protection against having a false-positive result survive in the literature. But the publication process that we have always been familiar with has made it very difficult to use replication attempts to their full advantage. It is, at least in part, because of these very problems that the COS and the OSF were created.

One of the best protections against capitalizing on chance is to be forced to state everything in advance of collecting the data. It is very difficult to capitalize on chance if you have to state in advance such things as exactly what hypothesis you will examine, exactly how you will examine it (what variables, operationalizations, conditions, and covariates you will use), how much data you will collect (no peeking in advance, and following a pre-determined termination rule), and exactly how you will analyze the data (what statistical tests on what variables with what covariates, if any). Of course, in order to not lose the value of exploratory research, you can always explore beyond the original, pre-determined plan. But such exploration has to be kept separate.

What the COS and the OSF have provided is a mechanism for doing all of that pre-determination in advance and "pre-registering" your study. On the OSF, pre-registering means that you, first, document all of the advance planning described above on the OSF. Then, pre-registering means that the entire project is frozen so that no one can change it—not even the original creator—before any data is collected. It is even possible for a journal to review the pre-registered plan, rather than a completed manuscript, and decide whether to give it provisional acceptance for publication in their journal. Thus, the publication decision is based on the importance of the research question and the quality of the method used to answer it. The publication decision is not, as it never should be, based on what the finding is. This, of course, relies on the research design being powerful enough so that if there is any reasonably large effect to be found, then the study has a high probability of finding it. But that, also, can be determined by the quality of the method being proposed to answer the question. The other part of the process of weeding out false-positives from the literature, direct replication, can also be facilitated by using the OSF to make materials, data, and analysis scripts openly available for anyone who wants to attempt a replication.

The reader is invited to become familiar with the COS and the OSF because of the many kinds of good work that they are doing. But, for purposes of this book, it should be apparent that part of that good work is to facilitate your research workflow in order to help you to become a more productive researcher, in spite of your many other responsibilities.

Open Source Software

In addition to automatic search alerts, bibliography software, and workflow resources, there are also software programs for collecting data, either in your own lab, or on a website. I will mention two such products briefly here, but they will be described in more detail in a subsequent chapter where they fit in appropriately. To collect data efficiently for some types of research questions, it can be useful to have the subject interact with a computer program, rather than directly with a live experimenter. There are several proprietary programs available for that purpose. But there is also a useful one called "OpenSesame" that is open source. Also, there is an online initiative called "OpenStax Tutor" that is specifically designed to not only serve as a resource for the student, but also to facilitate collecting data in research projects on student learning. Those products will be described in more detail in Chapter 3 and Chapter 4, respectively.

Summary

Finding ways to squeeze all of the tasks involved in doing research into a tightly packed, heavy teaching schedule is a challenge. However, by using techniques such as the overlapping independent studies strategy, using a spreadsheet to provide an item analysis of multiple-choice tests, and using conferences to pre-grade papers, you can increase your teaching efficiency without sacrificing quality. This will free up time that you can now devote to research. And to make the best use of that time, you can use digital resources such as automatic search alerts and Zotero bibliography software to automate finding and organizing the literature with which you need to stay current. Finally, your entire workflow, from designing, to data gathering, to analyzing and reporting can all be kept organized and secure against loss of files by using the Open Science Framework.

Suggested Readings

https://opensource.org/ The Open Source Initiative

> This not-for-profit organization promotes the development of software by and for the user. It maintains standards such as the definition of open source

to be used for open licensing. The purpose of the open model of developing software is to facilitate the best quality by engaging a whole community of developers and users.

https://osf.io/ The Open Science Framework

As described in this chapter, the OSF is an Internet-based tool for facilitating the entire workflow of the research process. It was built by and is maintained by the Center for Open Science. It continues to develop more and better features and is open to suggestions for improvement by its users.

References

Ioannidis, J. P. A. (2005). Why most published research findings are false. *PLoS Med, 2*(8), e124.

Kester, L., Kirschner, P. A., & van Merrienboer, J. J. G. (2004). Timing of information presentation in learning statistics. *Instructional Science: An International Journal of Learning and Cognition, 32*(3), 233–252.

Koedinger, K. R., Corbett, A. T., & Perfetti, C. (2012). The knowledge-learning-instruction framework: Bridging the science-practice chasm to enhance robust student learning. *Cognitive Science, 36*(5), 757–798.

Kornell, N., & Bjork, R. A. (2008). Learning concepts and categories: Is spacing the "Enemy of Induction"? *Psychological Science, 19*(6), 585–592.

Leinhardt, G. (1989). Math lessons: A contrast of novice and expert competence. *Journal for Research in Mathematics Education, 20*(1), 52–75.

McKoon, G., & Ratcliff, R. (1992). Spreading activation versus compound cue accounts of priming: Mediated priming revisited. *Journal of Experimental Psychology: Learning, Memory, and Cognition, 18*(6), 1155–1172.

Rohrer, D., & Taylor, K. (2007). The shuffling of mathematics problems improves learning. *Instructional Science: An International Journal of the Learning Sciences, 35*(6), 481–498.

Simmons, J. P., Nelson, L. D., & Simonsohn, U. (2011). False-positive psychology: Undisclosed flexibility in data collection and analysis allows presenting anything as significant. *Psychological Science, 22*(11), 1359–1366.

Sweller, J., & Cooper, G. A. (1985). The use of worked examples as a substitute for problem solving in learning algebra. *Cognition and Instruction, 2*(1), 59–89.

Taylor, K., & Rohrer, D. (2010). The effects of interleaved practice. *Applied Cognitive Psychology, 24*(6), 837–848.

3

OBTAINING SPACE AND EQUIPMENT RESOURCES

After Reading This Chapter You Will Know How to

- Improve your chances of obtaining external funding
- Be aware of possible pitfalls in choosing a research direction
- Use the modular strategy to conduct research on learning in real classroom settings
- Take advantage of opportunities to use the overlapping studies strategy
- Take advantage of open source software for experiment presentation

Introduction

Conducting research sometimes requires resources such as lab space or funding. These are resources that may be in short supply at a teaching institution. Therefore, if you are to obtain them at all you will at least have to build a case for why you need them. Furthermore, you will have to convince your administration that those resources will be well spent. In this chapter, we present the idea that "nothing succeeds like success." We will suggest ways to have early successes that can be used as evidence that you deserve greater resources to expand on them.

Even if some of the resources you wished you had are simply unavailable, then it may still be possible to build a successful research program by matching your research goals to the nature of the institution. Several examples of such a matching strategy will be presented, along with a detailed description of a design that lends itself to this strategy. Finally, this chapter will present several examples of successful use of the *overlapping independent studies* strategy that was introduced in Chapter 2.

Building a Case for Asking for More Resources

Obtaining space and other resources for your research is a process that may begin right with the process of obtaining an academic position. On the other hand, if you are already in an academic position in which the demands are now changing, it may be a process that will naturally occur as a result of those changes. If, once you have received an offer of a position, you are able to negotiate for some research space, such as a room to use as a lab to run subjects, or for a computer on which to analyze data, or for a startup budget to buy some equipment, then you should do so. However, the hiring committee (or the department chair) with which you are dealing may say that their institution simply does not have those kinds of resources to offer you. Or they might say that, if all goes as planned, they might have such resources in the future, but not now. Or they might say that such resources might be available at some time in the future, provided that you showed evidence that you really need them, and that you can make productive use of them.

I'll assume that you are in a position, or that you will be trying to obtain a position at an institution where, because they will be expecting you to conduct research, they would not say that they have absolutely nothing in the way of resources to offer you. On the other hand, I'll also assume that they are taking the position that because they are not a research university per se, the resources that they have to offer are quite scarce, and that you will have to prove yourself in order to be offered the opportunity to use them.

Matching Research Methods with the Available Resources

This puts you in the position in which you will have to find a way to begin with what you have, which might be very little. And yet you will have to build a case for asking for more. Thus, a good strategy would be to start conducting research that can reasonably be conducted with only the resources that you are starting with, but that, with the addition of some more resources, has the potential to be built into a more productive research program. You want to put yourself in the position to be able to get a publication out there, even if it is in a lower tier journal, to provide evidence of your capabilities, and to be able to argue that, if only you had better resources, you could conduct research that could be published in a more prestigious journal, thus enhancing the prestige of the institution.

You may not like the prospect that the direction of your research program is being influenced by such practical matters as what resources you have available, rather than by the importance of the research question, or your interest in it. But, remember, building the research program that you ultimately want to have will take some time. Your not being realistic at the beginning will not make that process go any faster. And it may even slow it down, or, at worst, you may give up.

Using Easy to Conduct Studies as a Way to Start

As an example of using the strategy described above, imagine that you could conduct your first experiment by recruiting subjects just by visiting classes and asking for volunteers, and your materials and procedure only involved presenting some stimulus materials in writing to your subjects and having them respond as a paper and pencil task. An example of such a situation could be asking a research question in the area of judgment and decision making, such as a question about the framing effect (Kahneman, 2003; Tversky & Kahneman, 1986). In such research, the stimulus materials can be a written scenario presenting a decision task framed in different ways and the subject's response is simply a choice between two alternatives. This particular phenomenon, the framing effect, has the advantage of being reliably reproducible. Of course, it has the disadvantage that it has already been thoroughly studied. This means that, in this particular case, you are not likely to come up with a new research question that would be so interesting as to get you published in a high tier journal. On the other hand, it does not mean that you couldn't come up with a research question that would be interesting enough to get published at all. Thus, such research could be an entry point for starting to provide the evidence you need of your research potential to enable you to begin arguing for better resources in the future. And, remember, this particular research area is only given as one example of many that you might find that have the useful characteristic of being able to be examined with limited resources.

Survey Research

Another example of a type of research that can be done with limited resources is research that can be done using a survey method. The survey instrument that you use might be one that has already been developed, or it might be one that you develop yourself. Some introductory psychology textbooks provided survey instruments that you can use. Finding such resources could be very time consuming for you. However, if you check with your publisher's representative to see what they might have to offer, they may be anxious to help you in order to improve the prospect of doing business with you. Therefore, they might be a resource that can save you many hours of your valuable time.

Once again, there might be an initial difficulty in finding a research question that you can examine using such resources, but that is also important enough to merit publication in a higher tier journal. But one can always start with trying to get published in a lower tier journal at first. The very fact that the resources initially available are only suitable to facilitate research that is publishable in lower tiered journals could eventually become part of the argument that more resources are needed in order to publish more impactful research.

In the case of surveys, the argument that might be able to be made is that there are survey instruments that could be used for more impactful research, but they are proprietary products that are relatively expensive. Or, another argument could be that what is needed is to develop a new survey instrument targeted to just the research question that you wanted to investigate. However, developing such an instrument would require research to establish the reliability and validity of the new instrument. The need for such research might provide the necessary fodder for an argument for departmental funds.

Seeking Internal Funding to Improve Your Chances of Obtaining External Funding

A possible strategy would be to argue that departmental funds, or some other kind of internal funding, ought to be made available to cover the costs of the kinds of research described above. The question may then arise as to why not seek external funding. That indeed might be a viable option. But it might not. An external funding agency may want to see some evidence of research productivity before considering your proposal. In that case, the argument might be able to be made that if departmental funds could be found to support an initial project, such support might be useful for increasing the prospects for obtaining external funding for a future project.

This raises the issue of another possible strategy. It might be the case that your eventual goal is to obtain external funding for some research that you want to conduct. However, you may find yourself in a position in which external funding agencies are less likely to be favorable toward a proposal from you because no one at your institution has previously received external funding from their agency. That may, in the minds of the decision makers at the external funding agency, call into question the likelihood of your being able to carry out your intended research project. However, they might look a little more favorably if they see that you have in the past convinced your department to provide you with internal funding for at least some pilot work leading toward the project for which you are applying for funds from the external agency. In such a situation, it might even be the case that your need for internal funding from your department for such pilot work is not really that great. However, just the fact that receiving such funding might have a positive influence on the external agency might, in itself, be a good reason to seek it.

The Road to Conducting Research on Teaching Methods

There is another type of research that lends itself particularly well to a situation in which resources are scarce. The reason resources are scarce is often because of the mission of the institution. Small private colleges, community colleges, and even large state universities that are either entirely or primarily four-year undergraduate teaching institutions typically have more of a teaching mission than a research mission. What could be more natural, then, at such institutions than to conduct research into effective teaching and learning?

What could be more important to an institution with a teaching mission than to help generate empirical support for methods that improve learning? It is important to note that what constitutes learning, from the point of view of an institution with such a mission, ought to include not just initial acquisition of to-be-learned material. It should also include later retention of the material, the ability to know when and how to apply it to practical situations, and the ability to transfer the knowledge from the context in which it was initially acquired to new and different contexts (Schmidt & Bjork, 1992).

From the point of view of the faculty member who needs to build and maintain a research program, studies in the acquisition and retention of knowledge have the advantage that they can be conducted using the faculty member's classes as a resource for recruiting the subjects and conducting the studies. Conducting studies in one's own classes has its own special challenges and opportunities. For example, some ethical issues arise because of the relationship between the faculty member, who is also the researcher, and the subjects, who are the researcher's students. Those issues will be covered in Chapter 6, where we talk about how to overcome bureaucratic stumbling blocks. However, on the plus side, there is now an Internet resource, OpenStax Tutor, which, although it is still under development at the time of this writing, may be a resource that you can find ways to use to facilitate conducting research on teaching and learning.

A special advantage of conducting research on teaching and learning in actual classroom settings is that there is currently a very great need for such research (Koedinger, Corbett, & Perfetti, 2012). As Koedinger et al. say in the abstract of their paper, "Despite the accumulation of substantial cognitive science research relevant to education, there remains confusion and controversy in the application of research to educational practice" (Koedinger et al., 2012, p. 757). That paper provides a great resource for ideas about important research questions that can often be addressed with limited resources.

For example, even though my initial graduate training involved doing research on verbalization and face recognition (Schooler, Ryan, & Reder, 1996), my research interests changed over time, and, partly due to practical concerns, eventually evolved into research on classroom teaching methods to improve learning. It was a gradual process of coming to the realization that in order to be a successful faculty member at a teaching institution, a good strategy would be to fit my research interests with the resources that were initially available to me, and which I was able to build on by using the strategies described above.

Although my master's level project during my graduate training, and subsequently, my first publications were, as indicated above, in the area of face recognition, for my dissertation project I turned to examining the role of self-explanation (Chi, de Leeuw, Chiu, & LaVancher, 1994) in transfer (Ryan, 1999). Here, I should offer some advice to graduate students, or undergraduate students contemplating moving on to graduate training. Think very carefully about what line of research you choose to pursue during your graduate training. Try to go in a direction that is the most likely to lead to solid, impactful publications while you are in graduate school. Be sure to work as hard as you can, while you have all of the resources of the university at which you are working for your doctorate available to you, to get those solid publications. If you do not, as was the case with me, you may find it much harder to get a research career off the ground, than would be the case had you gotten those solid publications. By having difficulty getting a research career off the ground, I mean that, first, your chances of obtaining a position at a major research university, at which research would be your main focus, will be lower. Also, although you may be able to obtain a position at a teaching university, you may find it harder to conduct research there, as is the whole point of this book. Thanks to my advisor, I was able to become a secondary author on a book chapter as my first publication (Schooler et al., 1996). However, given that that was my only publication during graduate school, the start of my academic career was, as you will see below, very rocky. Nevertheless, as the advice in this book is intended to illustrate, it is still possible to advance an academic career, but it could take longer and be more difficult.

My dissertation (Ryan, 1999) led to a line of research on issues of learning and using analogical reasoning for transfer. At the University of Pittsburgh, where I was trained, there was a large subject pool. There was a lab room that was dedicated solely to the research of my dissertation advisor, Jonathan Schooler, and his students. And, most importantly, once I had completed all of my course work, virtually all of my time was spent in research. The line of research that I had started in graduate school had been all laboratory experiments. However, once I had my first academic position, it was difficult to conduct laboratory experiments that investigated questions that were of enough interest to the field in a manner that was efficient enough to produce publications at a fast enough rate to be helpful to my career. I found myself in a position that had the very challenges that this book addresses.

The first academic position that I obtained was a one-year temporary position, that was later extended to a second year, at Slippery Rock University of Pennsylvania, one of the 14 state-owned, four-year undergraduate teaching universities in the Pennsylvania State System of Higher Education (PASSHE). During my two years there, I conducted laboratory research extending the dissertation research that I had done at the University of Pittsburgh. That dissertation research consisted of two experiments, but it had not led to a journal publication. I succeeded in completing a third experiment while I was at Slippery Rock, but was still unsuccessful at getting a manuscript presenting those three experiments published.

While at Slippery Rock University I engaged in a job search for a permanent position. Given my weak publication record, I was not able to obtain a position at a research university. However, I was able to obtain my first permanent academic position at Union College of Kentucky, in Barbourville, Kentucky. That college had no extra space for me to run subjects. It was a very small liberal arts college, at which the prospect of finding enough students who were intensely interested enough in conducting research to form a viable labor pool was very slim. I had some wonderful students there, three of whom actually produced a nice student research project by using students and people from the local community as subjects. They presented it at a small local undergraduate conference (Boles, Moorleghen, & Woods, 2000). Nevertheless, it was a situation in which I found it very difficult to produce anywhere near the amount and quality of data that I would need to produce to get another publication. Had I stayed there, and developed the kinds of strategies that we are promoting in this book, I may have been able to overcome that difficulty. However, during the two years I was at Union College, I and my dissertation advisor were able to finish a second publication, which, as it turned out, helped me to get the tenure track position that I have been in ever since (Ryan & Schooler, 1998).

After two years of job searching while at Union College, I was able to obtain a tenure track, assistant professor position here at Kutztown University of Pennsylvania, another of the PASSHE schools. They have provided me with some laboratory space in which to run subjects, but the time and labor involved with running them resulted in very slow production of data. The only labor that I had to run the subjects was my own and that of my undergraduate research assistants. My time was very limited due to the teaching load I carried, and that of my undergraduate research assistants was limited by their class load, and, in some cases, the need to work part time, or even full time, while attending college. Thus, I was able to produce enough data to put together a poster presentation, on average, once or twice a year, but, at first, I was not able to produce anything substantive enough to get a journal publication.

Over several years I was able to finish writing up the first of my two dissertation experiments, and to add further analysis of the data, which enabled me to publish those results (Ryan, 2005). However, up to that point, now that I was teaching full time, I was still not able to produce any new data by trying to do laboratory experiments that were worthy of journal publication. That is not to say that it is impossible to successfully conduct laboratory studies at a teaching university that can produce publishable data. It's just that, up to that point, I had not found an efficient way to do it. Instead, I needed a better strategy. As it turned out, that strategy was to turn to conducting research on applying some of the cognitive principles of learning that had been uncovered by the laboratory studies of others to actual classroom practice.

An Example of a Quasi-Experimental Study

That change of strategy actually occurred in two steps. First, I turned from trying to conduct laboratory studies on analogical reasoning and transfer, to considering research questions more directly related to accomplishing the kinds of real learning tasks involved in academic learning, rather than artificial laboratory tasks. In the second step, I moved to trying to find ways to conduct controlled, randomized trials, but still maintain fidelity to realistic classroom learning materials and methods.

Regarding the first step, in a graduate level statistics course I had been teaching I had developed a hands-on exercise to help the students understand the concept of the standard error of the mean. When I developed that teaching technique I had originally thought of it as only a possible way to improve my students' learning, but not as materials for a research study. But then it occurred to me that I could compare the performance on relevant test items of those students who had done the exercise to previous students, who had taken the exact same course without the exercise as a control group. Doing so would have the disadvantage that it was only a quasi-experimental design, and that, therefore, if the hands-on students outperformed the control students, there might be something other than the hands-on exercise that was responsible. On the other hand, such a study would have the advantage that because it examined actual classroom performance, it would have high ecological validity. It turned out that I was able to show an advantage of the hands-on group. Fortunately, I was able to argue that the difference was most likely due to the exercise. Using an analysis in which the test items were the unit of analysis (even though not when the students were the unit of analysis) the hands-on group performed significantly better on the test that covered the material with which the hands-on exercise was specifically designed to help. However, they did not perform better on the other tests. That finding was sufficiently interesting and impactful to lead to a publication in a fairly high tier journal (Ryan, 2006).

In the second step, I turned to trying to develop methods for conducting research on learning realistic, college level class material, using college students in actual classes as subjects, and comparing the relative effectiveness of various realistic classroom teaching methods. Trying to do this requires overcoming several problems that are specific to this kind of situation. One problem is how to make sure that conducting the experiment does not interfere with teaching the class to the extent that the students are being short changed. A specific instance of this problem is the ethical issue of how to randomly assign some students to an experimental condition that is expected to produce a benefit, and to assign others to a control condition, in which you do not expect them to receive that benefit. Another problem is that the professor teaching the course is also the researcher, which raises the possibility of conflicts of interest. How to handle that will be covered in Chapter 6 on overcoming bureaucratic hurdles.

Examples of Randomized Experiments

One way to accomplish random assignment is to randomly assign different sections of the same course to the different conditions. Doing so might be more feasible and acceptable for some situation than others. First, it requires that there be enough sections so that the random assignment has at least some reasonable chance of reducing the probability of a confound with such subject character-istics as prior knowledge and ability, or level of motivation. If such a strategy could be carried out over all of the universities in a reasonably large state system of universities, there might be a large enough group of sections so that the sec-tions, rather than individual students, could be used as the units of analysis. If that were the case, then the design would be a true experimental design in which a causal inference would be justified, rather than just a quasi-experimental design. It is likely that, even if all of the sections of a course over a whole state system were used, the sample size would still be relatively small compared to the sample size that would be obtained by using the individual students in a smaller number of sections as the unit of analysis. However, by using the section as the unit of analysis, you are averaging across all the individual students in each section. This might result in section averages that had considerably low variability within each condition. That variability might be even lower than what you could achieve within each condition by using the individual students from just a few sections as the units of analysis. If so, then the strategy of using all of the sections across the whole state system could result in a more statistically powerful experiment than one conducted within one university.

Of course, obtaining the cooperation of the instructors and administrations of all of the universities in a state system might be quite a feat for even a seasoned veteran researcher, let alone someone just starting out. Furthermore, if your aca-demic position is not in such a state system, then the above described strategy is not available to you. Therefore, let's consider next a different strategy, and one that might be applicable to a situation in which only one section of a course is available. Rather than requiring multiple sections, this strategy only requires a reasonably large number of individual students, whether from a small number of sections, or even from only one. That strategy involves alternating the experimen-tal and control conditions across different modules within a course.

In any given course the instructor typically has a set of learning objectives and, at least in some cases, these would correspond with modules, or topics, to be covered in the course. When using the strategy of randomly assigning students to experimental and control conditions, the problem arises that there might be an a priori hypothesis that the experimental condition will benefit more than the con-trol condition. Thus, there arises the question of whether it is ethical to randomly assign some students to a condition in which you are hypothesizing that they will not learn as well as if they had been assigned to the other condition. One possible answer to this ethical question might be to draw on the fact that the differential benefits are only hypothesized. That is, they are not known to be actual. In sup-port of this position, one could point out that if one were already confident that the differential benefits existed, then the experiment would not be being carried out. The situation could be considered analogous to a medical trial in which a treatment, the effectiveness of which was being tested, is withheld from a control group. But once the data begins to convincingly support the relatively greater effectiveness of the experimental treatment, it is no longer ethical to continue to provide it to some subjects while withholding it from others. Given that the hope of the researcher is to provide evidence that the experimental treatment is more effective, it is disingenuous to rely on that argument if a better strategy can be found. Fortunately, the strategy of alternating the experimental and control conditions across different modules within a course, which we will call the *modular strategy*, provides such a better strategy, although it is not without its own problems.

The Modular Strategy

In the modular strategy you select two, or some multiple of two, topics within a course to use to compare two different teaching methods. It is important, as will be seen below, that the topics are of as equal difficulty as possible, and that they are as equal as possible in terms of their importance for the course. For a simple example, let's assume that you are using just two topics, which we will call Topic 1 and Topic 2. You then randomly divide your students into two groups. We'll call them Group A and Group B. You could also create groups A and B by forming matched pairs based on some important subject variable such as their general level of academic aptitude (as measures by their current GPA), or whatever other subject variable you deemed important for maximizing the similarity of your two groups. Then, when Topic 1 is being taught, you randomly assign one of the groups to be taught that module by the experimental method, and the other by the control method. For Topic 2, you counterbalance by reversing which group is taught by which method. This has the advantage that each group is taught the same number of topics by the experimental method and the control method. Therefore, even though you are teaching some of the time by a method that you hypothesize is better, and some of the time by a method that you hypothesize is not as good, your subjects all receive the same distribution of better and poorer methods, although on different topics. That is why it is important that the two topics should not be of unequal importance for the course.

If you like visual representations, you can think of this as a checkerboard design. I like to think of the two rows of two squares as each row being a different topic. That matches up with a schedule of topics on a syllabus having different topics on different rows. Then the two groups of subjects can be thought of as two columns. Just remember that those two columns represent two groups of subjects, but not two conditions. In this representation, the conditions can be represented by the colors. For example, the experimental condition can be the black squares of the checkerboard, and the control condition can be the red squares.

When you analyze the data, one thing you can do is a separate comparison of the performance between conditions for each topic (you are doing one *t* test between the left and right squares at each row). Those comparisons are between subjects. For each test you are relying on the groups being equivalent enough in ability so that you don't have to worry about a confound with their ability calling the results into question in either test. Thus, if you could have formed matched pairs, that would have been better than just random assignment.

You can also do separate comparisons of the performance between conditions for each group (you are doing one *t* test between the top and bottom squares at each column). Those comparisons are within subjects. In this case, however, you are relying on the topics being equivalent enough in difficulty so that you don't have to worry about a confound with their ability calling the results into question in either test.

With this design, the cleanest way to test your hypothesis is to do both of the pairs of tests described above. If you try to combine the data and do a factorial ANOVA, you can do so, but you run into the problem that the design is a fractional Latin square. It might not be easy to find a statistical program that has a fractional Latin square design as one of your choices. However, there are two other possibilities, although the complete details of how to do them are beyond the scope of this book. First, you may be able to analyze such a design by learning enough about using a script or syntax file to do it. On the other hand, it may be actually easier to simply do the analysis by hand, and the explanation below may facilitate your ability to do so.

There are three factors, each with two levels. The factors are conditions, topics, and groups (of subjects). If you try to combine them into a three factor ANOVA, then the condition factor is completely confounded with the topic by group interaction (your statistical program might say they are aliased). The topic factor is completely confounded with the condition by group interaction, and the group factor is completely confounded with the condition by topic interaction. Therefore, you can conduct the analysis as a 2 (groups—between subjects) by 2 (topics—within subjects) analysis. In that analysis, the within subjects groups by topics interaction is actually the condition factor.

Of course the strategy of using a large number of sections over several universities and the strategy of using the modular checkerboard approach, within as little as one section, are only two examples among many others that could be used. They were presented as two extremes, between which there are many possible variations. For example, at my university I was able to engage the cooperation of several of my colleagues in order to conduct research within all (or in some semesters, almost all) of the eight sections of statistics in our department.

During the last several years I have been conducting studies using the statistics students at our university as subjects. As mentioned above, using students in a class that you yourself teach raises some tactical ethical issues that will be discussed in Chapter 6. Those studies have produced data that has been presented at several conferences as posters. They comprise a series of studies that are still going on at this writing, and are intended to produce one manuscript describing all of them for journal submission. I had mentioned those studies in Chapter 2, where I pointed out that initially I was not finding convincing evidence to support the original hypothesis. Therefore, I can point to them as only a partial success as yet.

However, there is one particular study in the series that used a method that I have not yet described. Also, during the time I was conducting that series, the overlapping independent studies strategy was leading to other studies and other successes for me and for my students. I will next describe one of the studies in the statistics series that used a method that I have not yet described, and then I will describe the other overlapping studies that occurred during the same time I was conducting the statistics series, but were independent of them. Three of those studies led to successful publications for me and my students.

Using an LMS to Conduct a Study

I happened to be commiserating with a colleague about the difficulty of doing research using statistics students as subjects without using up too much class time for the experimental activities. As I mentioned above, the series of statistics studies that I had been conducting were not leading to convincing evidence that interleaving examples improved learning which statistical procedure to apply to a given research situation. Fortunately, because my automatic search alerts had turned up the paper about the Knowledge-Learning-Instruction framework (KLI), which was briefly described in Chapter 2, I was able to focus my statistics research on some factors other than interleaving. Those factors would have the potential to improve the kind of learning that I was interested in improving. However, I was still especially concerned about two results. First, even when there was evidence that one of the factors from the KLI framework (focusing the learners on the features of the categories to be learned) was significantly more beneficial than a control condition, it was difficult to get the improvements up to absolute levels of performance that would be acceptable as a grade in an academic course (i.e., up to at least 60 percent correct). Second, even when performance was brought up to such a level on a test given immediately after the learning activity, the performance fell back down to academically unacceptable levels on a retention test given only a few weeks later.

Given these concerns, I had an idea for a study that would examine the effects of two factors suggested by the KLI framework that I had not previously tried. One was spacing of the study sessions, and the other was practicing retrieval of the material to be learned. However, the reason I was commiserating with my colleague was because I needed a way to use those factors in an ecologically valid study in a classroom, but without using up too much of the teaching time. My colleague suggested the idea of creating study materials that could be presented on our learning management system (LMS) as homework assignments that could be done by the students outside of class time. This solved the problem of eating up teaching time during the class, and, in addition, automated the data collection process. Two birds with one stone!

I should point out here yet another benefit that occurred by using the LMS method of administering the experiment. This is actually a variation on the multiple overlapping independent lines of research idea. While the experimental subjects were doing their task, there was a need for some cognitively equivalent task for the control subjects. One of my other experiments (which will be described below) had raised a question about a possible misconception about algebra from which students might suffer. For my control condition in the spacing of study and practicing retrieval experiment in statistics, I used a task that examined the question about the possibility that the students suffered from the misconception that had been raised by the other overlapping independent experiment. And, once again, this was done without taking up any teaching time, and the data collection was automated! (Four birds with one stone?)

Four Overlapping Studies, Three Leading to Publication, One of Which Was in *Science*

As mentioned above, the series of statistics studies have, as yet, produced some data that was disappointing, and some that has some promise, but needs more work. Those studies are still ongoing and may yet lead to a publication. But in the meanwhile there were four other studies going on which overlapped the statistics series. One was inspired by another paper that I had run across as the result of my automatic search alerts. I will describe that one first. Next I will describe the other three. Those three all led to publications, two in lower tier journals, and one in *Science*.

The Problem Format Study

In my automatic search alerts, I had several searches that were on keywords. Some were related to my previous interest in using analogical reasoning in learning mathematics, and some were related to my more recent interests in applying cognitive method to educational practice. One of my search alerts simply lets me know whether there are any new publications by Ken Koedinger, a researcher whose work I have drawn on more than once. Here might be a good place to relate a story about something that happened when I was in graduate school. It was seemingly just a chance encounter, but it pointed my career in a direction that it continued to follow ever since. It was right at the point in my graduate school career at which I had finished my master's level project and was trying to decide on a direction for my dissertation. I was, as explained earlier in this chapter, considering examining how self-explanation might be related to transfer. I was interested in specifically how explanations that formed analogies might influence transfer. For learning and transfer materials I was considering using some kinds of artificial laboratory materials that had been used in earlier studies of analogical reasoning. I happened to be headed to lunch with some colleagues somewhere in Oakland (the section of Pittsburgh in which both the University of Pittsburgh and Carnegie Mellon University [CMU] are located).

We met some other colleagues from Carnegie Mellon who were also headed to lunch, and so we walked together and talked. Among the colleagues from CMU was Ken Koedinger, who was a post-doc at the time, and whose work I've cited here. I was explaining my thoughts on what might be a good idea for my dissertation. I was hoping, of course, to pick the brains of my more eminent colleagues. When I explained my idea of examining self-explanations that formed an analogy between the underlying structures of two sets of learning materials, Ken offered the suggestion that I ought to try algebra problems as the learning materials, instead of the artificial laboratory materials that I was thinking of using. He explained that even though the artificial materials had been used successfully in previous research, algebra was a more ecologically valid task, and might be of greater interest to people in the field of education, as well as cognitive psychology, and thus it might be easier to publish my research. Although I'll never know for sure whether conducting research using the algebra materials turned out better than if I had stuck to the artificial laboratory materials, I do believe that going in the direction of research that can be efficiently conducted in a teaching setting has made me more productive than I would have been otherwise.

Now, back to the automatic search alert. This one turned up a recent paper in which the format in which mathematical problems were presented, whether as a word problem, or whether as one of several ways of presenting the problem as an equation, influenced students' success at solving them (Koedinger, Alibali, & Nathan, 2008). On reading that paper I not only saw some new possible questions that it raised, but I also realized that implementing an experiment to examine those questions would be exceptionally easy. It only amounted to writing up the same mathematical problem in different formats and putting them on separate sheets of paper. Then an undergraduate volunteers research assistant would only have to recruit subjects through our subject pool (to be described in Chapter 4) and present one of the sheets, randomly chosen, to the subject. The only possible complications in the procedure would be to instruct the subject that they were allowed to use a calculator, but that we needed them to write down their work as individual steps so that we could see exactly what they did, and in what order. Because the main dependent variable would be the percentage of subjects who were successful in each format, it could require more subjects to get a significant result than if the dependent variable were an interval/ratio quantitative measure. But because the procedure was so simple, and running each subject took so little time, it was feasible to collect relatively large quantates of data in a relatively short time. Furthermore, the simplicity of the procedure saved time in another way as well. Often the amount of labor required from me to run a study comes from the time I need to put in to train my research assistants. With this study, there was almost no training required.

The study examining the effects of different equation formats ended up being a series of three studies. They produced some conference presentations as posters, which enabled me to give the research assistants involved experience attending a conference. Also, this is the study that led to the question that was addressed in the control condition of the experiment described above that was presented to our statistics students in an automated fashion on our LMS.

I would like to point out briefly here that in my descriptions of my research I have referred to a research practice that, in the past, was considered standard, but is now being considered questionable. I am referring to my saying that I needed to run enough subjects to obtain significant results. Some people in psychology, as well as in other fields of science, are of the opinion that we need to look at our research in ways that go beyond obtaining statistically significant results. They point out that in a field like psychology, where the phenomena we study have a tremendously large number of factors all interacting and contributing to the variability of whatever we are studying, it may be the case that the statistical concept of a null hypothesis may never be the reality. Instead, a more reasonable question than, "Is there any effect at all?" might be, "Given that there is probably always some effect, however small, is the effect large enough to be of any real theoretical interest or practical usefulness?" Others would say that there may be the possibility of an effect existing or not existing. But they would say that a researcher should never design a study for the purpose of "Showing that X affects Y." Rather, the unbiased way to ask the question would be to design a study to answer the question "Does X affect Y or does it not?" In this case, you could also include the idea that maybe some effect, however small, always exists, and modify the question to "Does X affect Y to any interesting or practically important degree, or does it not?" In any event, to change our research practices to be more in line with the unbiased approach that scientists have always said they support, there are ways in which our research practices (and our journal publication practices) need to be modified. A full discussion of this topic is outside the scope of this book. The reader is encouraged to become familiar with the work of the Center for Open Science (COS; https://cos.io/) for a full understanding of these issues (some of the good work being done by the COS was described in Chapter 2). Let it just be said here that better research practices would include supplementing significance tests with confidence intervals and measures of effect size, and, as described in Chapter 2, preregistering research plans, thus allowing journals to decide on which studies to publish based on the importance of the research question and the soundness of the method being used to answer it, rather than on which result was found.

The study examining the effects of different equation formats has not yet led to a journal publication. The data from it, as the data from the statistics studies is all "in the pipeline." Although that may sound like some sort of backup that would not be a good thing, let me point out that having data in the pipeline is a natural part of the overlapping independent studies strategies. As an example of the value of having such data, there was data from my second dissertation experiment that was sitting in that pipeline literally for years before it eventually led to a publication. When it did, it enabled one of my especially talented research assistants to obtain authorship on a journal publication before he even attended graduate school. I'll get to that story soon. But first, I want to describe an example of how the overlapping independent studies strategy again worked to my advantage, as well as to the advantage of several of my research assistants, two of whom, like the one mentioned above, obtained authorship on a journal publication with only an undergraduate education.

The Internet Research versus Lab Research Study

This story starts out in a way that does not sound like it would lead to much that would enhance an academic career. Yet it ended up producing several conference presentations, gave several undergraduate volunteer research assistants experience at presenting at those conferences, and eventually led to a journal publication for me and two of those research assistants. The story began with me having a dry spell in my research activity. I had conducted some experiments that had not produced useful data (according to the new approaches being advocated by the COS they were experiments that were not sufficiently thought out to start with). I needed to work on developing some better ideas. But in the meantime, I had several undergraduate research assistants who needed something to work on. Then a strange thought occurred to me. I had always heard that research ideas can come from anywhere, including from your personal experiences. I felt as though I was really scraping the bottom of the barrel, but here it is.

Among the various house insects that one encounters, there is one that I have always found particularly objectionable, the house centipede. This is an insect that can grow to about an inch and a half, maybe two inches, long. It has multiple legs, but unlike a garden centipede, whose legs are short, the house centipede's legs are long. Sometimes the legs are striped. One could even look at this insect as resembling a pretty feather. And yet, every time I see one, I have a primitive, automatic fear and revulsion reaction. My only thought is that this thing must die, and as soon as possible. However, as a good scientist, I was able to use this aversive experience as a source of a possible research question. My question was, what exactly is it about this insect that makes me want to kill it? Is it that I find it frightening, or is it that I find it disgusting? Emotion is not my area of research, but I know that fear and disgust, although related, are two different emotions.

And so, I proposed to my research assistants that they could design and carry out an experiment to answer the question, "What makes people react with hostility toward an insect? Is it the insect's frighteningness, its disgustingness, or both?" To answer this question, the research assistants first had to collect pictures of insects and have independent subject judges rate them on their frighteningness and on their disgustingness. Then, using those ratings, we selected insects that varied independently on those two dimensions. Finally, we presented those pictures to new subjects who rated how much they wanted to kill the insect (or have it killed for them, in case they didn't want to get near it due to its disgustingness).

This project was intriguing to my research assistants (and to me). It kept them busy learning much about the nuts and bolts of doing research. Even before they got to the second part of the experiment they were able to produce a poster presentation on the various different characteristics of the insects that were associated with their being rated as either highly frightening or highly disgusting. But when we got to the part where we had to collect the hostility ratings, another thought occurred to me. At one of the annual conventions of the Association for Psychological Science (APS) that I had been to one spring, I had attended a workshop on how to write Javascript programs to collect data from the Internet. I thought that that would be a viable way to collect the hostility ratings and to get a large quantity of data. So, I spent the summer following that conference reading a book by the workshop's presenter, corresponding with him by email, and learning how to write the Javascript code to present my hostility experiment online. When I put it up online, in the first week I got 278 subjects' data. In the first month, I had 634, and after 10 months I had 1525.

But, of course, a question that arose was whether the data collected from the Internet was trustworthy. Therefore, I put my research assistants to work conducting the same study that I had conducted via the Internet in a face-to-face manner. They did that in two ways. Part of the data was collected face-to-face in one of our labs via a paper and pencil administration. Another part of the data was collected by having subjects come to the lab and run themselves through the experiment on a computer, doing the Internet version of the experiment, but in the presence of one of my research assistants. Thus, we now had data that was collected both with and without any personal interaction with a human experimenter. The findings in both administrations had the same patterns in the data. In the human interaction data, which contained data from 180 subjects, there were significant main effects of frighteningness, disgustingness, and gender, as well as some nonsignificant interactions involving gender. In the Internet only data, which contained data from 1301 subjects after the data were cleaned, the exact same patterns occurred, except that all of them were statistically significant (Ryan, Wilde, & Crist, 2013).

Two of my research assistants had done more than just run subjects in the lab. They had also conducted a literature search on research comparing Internet studies to lab studies, and they helped me to write the paper. Therefore, they earned secondary authorship. So, in the end, a study that had begun as just a mechanism to keep my research assistants busy with something that they would find interesting, and from which they could learn something about the nuts and bolts of conducting research, ended up resulting in a journal publication for them and for me.

The Long Road to Publishing the Second Dissertation Study

I now turn to the example of how having patience with allowing data to stay in the pipeline until an opportunity arises to do something with it can pay off. After

I finished my two dissertation experiments and successfully defended my dissertation, my efforts to get them published as a single journal article were frustrating. At first, I sent the manuscript describing the two experiments, perhaps overoptimistically, to a major psychology journal. The reviewers were helpful, but this was my first experience with being reviewed, and, since some readers may be in the position of not having had that experience, let me describe it for you.

A review starts off with the editor's summary of what they perceive to be your aims in the paper. Then they provide their overall assessment. Theoretically, that could be something like, "We are so happy to receive this wonderful, insightful work, and are anxious to publish it to enlighten the world with its groundbreaking new findings." Theoretically it could say that. But I doubt that ever happens. It has certainly never happened to me. At the other end of the spectrum, again theoretically, it could say something like, "What a piece of trash. How dare you waste our time with it. Go back to selling shoes." But even if you submit something terrible they would never be so unprofessional as to say something like that. If they are really not interested in your manuscript, they will say something like, "Thank you for considering our journal for your manuscript. However, it does not fit with our needs at this time." They may also suggest another type of journal at which they believe you might have more success. If it is poorly written, they might add, "This manuscript could benefit from substantial rewriting to improve its mechanics and readability." The suggestion of other journals is a sincere attempt to help you get published. The suggestion of "substantial rewriting" is a polite way of saying that, at least at this time, you are out of your league. In other words, even though the prospect of sending that first manuscript out may be scary, be aware that the journal editors and reviewers are professionals who, although they expect you to do your part, also understand what it's like to try to get started in the field and are willing, as much as they reasonably can, to help you.

If your manuscript has some potential, then the editor has to decide whether it has enough potential to ask some of their colleagues to devote some of their valuable time to reviewing it. Bear in mind that reviewers are professionals who volunteer their time to do this valuable work, and when you are starting out you should be grateful for their help, even though it is sometimes painful to hear their opinion. Suppose, in the reviewer's opinion, the manuscript needs much work, as was the case with my first submission. If so, after the initial summary, the assessment of the editor might be something like, "This manuscript may have the potential to contribute to the field, but the author needs to become more familiar with the pertinent previous literature. We might be able to reconsider a manuscript along these lines, but the author needs to do more empirical work and to do a better job of situating it within the current literature." Then, given that the manuscript was sent out to reviewers (there are usually three of them), the editor will briefly give you the final assessment of each reviewer.

Typically, one reviewer is pretty favorable. I think what happens there is that the editor may be breaking in a colleague who is new to the field as a reviewer and that colleague feels as if they aren't yet well established enough to be too hard on the submitter. That reviewer will probably support publishing your work, but will have a numbered list of several requests for various improvements. Another reviewer will be just as tough as the first one was lenient. They might even go as far as to suggest not publishing your manuscript. Nevertheless, they will also provide a list of comments. Then the third reviewer may go down the middle, suggesting that your work *might* be suitable for publication, provided you can successfully address their numbered list of comments. The editor will then instruct you that you may revise and resubmit your manuscript. They will also tell you that with your manuscript to be sure to submit a cover letter in which you address the reviewers' comments. The reason the reviewers number their comments is because you are expected to address each and every one of them. They want to make sure you don't "inadvertently" skip any. You are permitted to disagree with a comment, but you had better have a strong argument to support your disagreement.

When I submitted the manuscript describing my two dissertation experiments, the first major journal to which I submitted it basically suggested I should try another journal. The second journal was willing to accept a revised resubmission, but expected more empirical work. In other words, two experiments were not enough. It was at that point that I had just accepted my first academic position, as mentioned earlier, at a state university as a one-year temporary faculty, which later was extended to a second year. During that time I managed to conduct a third experiment. It was from that experience that I quickly learned how different it is to try to conduct an experiment at a teaching university compared to a research university. Nevertheless, I conducted the experiment and added it to the manuscript. I now had a much longer manuscript that I needed to send to my co-author, my dissertation advisor. Given that this was my first attempt at taking the lead in writing a manuscript, I must confess that it was not only too long, but not an easy read. My advisor, bless his heart, made several attempts to get to it, but finally admitted to me that he just couldn't get through it. His suggestion was to send just the first experiment off to a journal in which he believed I had a better chance of getting published as a single author publication. He also had some suggestions for the second experiment, and he suggested I might consider just jettisoning the third. I should point out that I recognize that his advice might be seen as amounting to suggesting that I engage in piecemeal publication, a practice that is frowned on. However, in our defense, I will point out that piecemeal publication is considered unethical because it can be used as a mechanism to inflate your number of publications if you merely break up a manuscript and submit each part to a different journal. I did more than just break up that long manuscript. One of the suggestions of that first review was to dig further into the data from my first experiment, code my subjects' responses for partial credit on their answers to my algebra problems, and analyze that partial credit data. So, I followed that instruction to improve the description of the first experiment before submitting all of those results to the journal suggested by my advisor. However, I still had the data from the second experiment, and it too could be recoded for partial credit to provide a deeper analysis of my subjects' responses.

I didn't want to try submitting the second dissertation experiment without doing the same kind of partial credit analysis as had been done for the first experiment. There was also a large amount of other data about individual subject characteristics that had been collected, but never coded or analyzed. This data included the subject's gender, how long ago they took their most recent algebra course, their verbal and math SAT scores, their GPAs, and their score on a vocabulary test that we were using as a proxy for an IQ score. I had obtained an internal grant to pay a work-study graduate student to do the partial credit scoring. I also had an especially talented undergraduate volunteer research assistant who had already made several other contributions to my future research plans. He contributed to the manuscript by coding and analyzing all of the individual subject data. Furthermore, he did some additional literature searching beyond what I had originally done, and contributed some ideas for the discussion section of the manuscript. Thus, that research assistant obtained authorship on that manuscript.

The story of how my second dissertation experiment eventually made it to publication illustrates the importance of dogged persistence. I had suffered some defeats along the way, but had I given up on that data I would have gone further down the road of becoming a teacher who needs to do research to advance his career, but fails to do so because of the perceived difficulty of the challenge.

The Reproducibility Project: Psychology (RPP)

I now turn to an example of how just keeping an eye out for opportunities can have unexpected benefits. This is the last of the four studies that overlapped the continuing studies of statistics learning in actual classrooms. This opportunity arose as a result of following the work of the COS.

I came across the COS in an email. I don't even remember what exactly that first email was about. However, as I learned more about the COS I became very interested in their work. One of the projects that they initiated was the Reproducibility Project: Psychology (RPP). In it they proposed to have collaborators in psychological science from around the world conduct direct replication attempts for 100 psychology findings published in 2008 in three major psychology journals. I had joined a Google group to stay abreast of what they were doing. As a result, I was receiving the emails regarding the RPP. In one email, they announced that the possible projects for replication were now listed in a spreadsheet so that anyone interested could look through them and claim one of the projects for their lab to try to replicate. When I looked through them and saw what would be involved in trying to conduct one of these replications I decided that trying to do so would be beyond the scope of what I could do. The replications were to follow a strict protocol. It involved such things as engaging the original authors in cooperating by providing all of their original materials and methods, and giving their stamp of approval for the replication. The replication plan had to be prereg-istered. Replicating authors were to audit one another's plans to verify fidelity to the original study. And there was a deadline to get all the work done so that it could be written up for journal submission in a timely manner. Given my lack of labor resources due to my teaching load and other responsibilities, I saw no way that I could make such a commitment. Nevertheless, I followed the progress of the project with great interest.

Then, one day there was an email broadcast to the whole group in which one of the replicating authors was asking for help with some statistical analysis. He needed help with calculating confidence intervals on effect sizes from ANOVAs. Given that I had taught statistics for years, was doing research in learning statistics, and had even done a little statistical consulting, this email especially caught my interest. I knew how to calculate confidence intervals around a mean or a dif-ference between means. I knew how to calculate various measures of effect size, including for ANOVAs. I had never calculated a confidence interval around an effect size before, but how hard could it be? Furthermore, I surmised that this researcher would probably receive offers from many other researchers from around the world who were at least as qualified, if not more qualified, as I. Therefore, even though I responded to the email offering my services, I actually did not expect to be taken up on my offer. Surprise. I got an email right back thanking me for the offer, and sending me the necessary data and further information about what was needed. Given that I did not actually know how to calculate confidence intervals around effect sizes from an ANOVA I did the most logical thing. I Googled it.

Fortunately, there were reputable sources on the Internet that provided detailed information that I could use, along with examples, and even analysis scripts that would just need to be modified for the data to be analyzed. However, it was not a quick, easy, or straightforward process. It was a good bit of work that required several steps. Nevertheless, it was fortunate that this occurred during the summer, during the second half of which I was not teaching, and so I was able to devote the time to get the project done. I made notes for myself as I worked and I saved all of the relevant files. When I was done, I sent it off to the requesting author. Then the fall semester began. Now I was busy with teaching again and I actually completely forgot about that project.

I continued to follow the progress of the RPP. At one point I received an email saying the project was in the process of being written up, and that all of the collaborating authors needed to check a spreadsheet containing their names and affiliations, and the project on which they had worked, and they needed to verify that it was all correct. At first I assumed that this was an email that had gone to the whole Google group, even though only the collaborating authors needed to act on it. Then I realized that the way the email was written, it seemed to be addressed just to the authors. That made me wonder why I had received it. So, I clicked on the link to the spreadsheet and began scrolling through the names. Sure enough, there I was. At that point, I honestly did not remember that I had contributed anything and thought that it might be an error. Then I had this vague memory that I had done something over the summer having something to do with helping with statistics. I had to check through my files to see exactly what it was. When I saw the records of all the work I had done I realized that I had indeed made a larger contribution than I originally remembered. To my surprise and delight, the future emails about the RPP said that the manuscript describing the project was being submitted to *Science*. So, in spite of my not being in anywhere near a position to tackle a direct replication attempt for the project due to my being a faculty member at a teaching institution with a heavy teaching load and other responsibilities, because of taking a chance on an opportunity that I initially believed to have a slim chance of working out, I ended up with contributing authorship on a paper published in one of the world's top journals (Open Science Collaboration, 2015). To be clear, I am only one of 270 contributing authors to the collaboration, but I'll take it.

Conducting research on teaching and learning in order to match your research methods with the resources available at a teaching university, and watching for opportunities on which to capitalize are useful strategies for building a research program when you are starting out with scarce resources. However, in order to expand your ability to conduct research into areas beyond questions about teaching methods and learning you may wish to conduct experiments on other types of questions that require presenting stimulus materials and collecting responses using software. There are many software packages available for that purpose, most of which are proprietary. However, there is a good open source package called OpenSesame. Comprehensive information about that package can be found at http://osdoc.cogsci.nl/. However, I'll provide a brief description here.

OpenSesame has the advantage that it is open source. Thus, it is not only available for anyone to download for free from the Internet, but also, if you know how to and wish to alter it to suit your needs, there is nothing preventing you from doing so. If you then wish to offer your alteration to contribute to its development, you can do that also.

OpenSesame is available to download and to run on all the major computer platforms. It can run on Windows, Mac, or Linux. It enables the user to build his or her own program to present an experiment to subjects and collect their data. Fortunately, for the user who knows little or no computer programming, it has a graphical interface in which you can build your experiment by making selections via checkboxes and drop down menus. It provides you with plenty of ways to get help and even includes example experiments, which can be very helpful in figuring out how to use the software if you are new to using this type of program.

OpenSesame can be used not only to build experiments to run yourself, it can also be used by students in a class like experimental psychology to construct programs to collect data for their class projects. If a student has an especially good project in mind, it can be a tool that might enable him or her to conduct an experiment that he or she can then submit to an undergraduate conference or an undergraduate journal. And, if it is advanced enough, it might even enable a student or group of students to conduct an experiment that they could submit to a professional conference or even a professional journal.

Summary

Building a successful research program in an institution that does not readily supply resources such as lab space and funding can still be accomplished. One way to do this is to start with small successes that justify spending scarce and therefore precious resources on your research program. Even if that is not possible, there are still ways to increase research productivity in a low resource environment. Examples are making use of your LMS as a platform to gather data, using the overlapping independent studies strategy, and using open source software for data collection.

Suggested Readings

https://cos.io/ Center for Open Science

> The Center for Open Science (COS) is a not for profit organization founded in 2013 to promote and facilitate openness in science. One of its most important and useful initiatives is the Open Science Framework. It is funded by several philanthropic foundations as well as other organizations and private donors.

http://osdoc.cogsci.nl/ OpenSesame

> OpenSesame is open source software for conducting experiments in psychology and other disciplines. It is available for Windows, Mac OS, Linux, and it even has a runtime interface for Android. The program comes with example experiments to help the user learn the program or to use as a basis to construct your own experiment by modifying the example. At the website above you can download and install the program, or read tutorials.

References

Chi, M. T. H., de Leeuw, N., Chiu, M.-H., & LaVancher, C. (1994). Eliciting self-explanations improves understanding. *Cognitive Science*, *18*(3), 439–477.

Kahneman, D. (2003). A perspective on judgment and choice: Mapping bounded rationality. *American Psychologist*, *58*(9), 697–720.

Koedinger, K. R., Alibali, M. W., & Nathan, M. J. (2008). Trade-offs between grounded and abstract representations: Evidence from algebra problem solving. *Cognitive Science*, *32*(2), 366–397.

Koedinger, K. R., Corbett, A. T., & Perfetti, C. (2012). The knowledge-learning-instruction framework: bridging the science-practice chasm to enhance robust student learning. *Cognitive Science*, *36*(5), 757–798.

Open Science Collaboration. (2015). Estimating the reproducibility of psychological science. *Science, 349*(6251), aac4716.

Ryan, R. S. (1999). *The role of self-examination in adapting as well as transferring a solution procedure.* Ann Arbor, MI: ProQuest Information & Learning.

Ryan, R. S. (2005). Judging similarity facilitates deriving a new solution procedure. *Cognitive Technology, 10*(2), 5–12.

Ryan, R. S. (2006). A hands-on exercise improves understanding of the standard error of the mean. *Teaching of Psychology, 33*(3), 180–183.

Ryan, R. S., & Schooler, J. W. (1998). Whom do words hurt? Individual differences in susceptibility to verbal overshadowing. *Applied Cognitive Psychology, 12*(Spec. Issue), S105–S125.

Ryan, R. S., Wilde, M., & Crist, S. (2013). Compared to a small, supervised lab experiment, a large, unsupervised web-based experiment on a previously unknown effect has benefits that outweigh its potential costs. *Computers in Human Behavior, 29*(4), 1295–1301.

Schmidt, R. A., & Bjork, R. A. (1992). New conceptualizations of practice: Common principles in three paradigms suggest new concepts for training. *Psychological Science, 3*(4), 207–217.

Schooler, J. W., Ryan, R. S., & Reder, L. M. (1996). The costs and benefits of verbally rehearsing memory for faces. In *Basic and Applied Memory Research* (Vol. 2: Practical Application, pp. 51–56). Mahwah, NJ: Erlbaum.

Tversky, A., & Kahneman, D. (1986). Rational choice and the framing of decisions. *The Journal of Business, 59*(4), S251–S278.

4

FINDING AVAILABLE HUMAN SUBJECTS

After Reading This Chapter You Will Know How to

- Recruit from a colleague's class
- Overcome the hurdles of recruiting from your own classes
- Use a bulletin board-based subject pool system
- Make use of an Internet-based subject pool system
- Recognize and deal with the challenges of conducting research on a Learning Management System (LMS)

Introduction

Researchers in the social and behavioral sciences most often use human subjects for their research. It is possible to recruit subjects from classes, either your own or a colleague's. However, there are special challenges to each tactic, such as the ethical problems associated with asking for voluntary participation from students when you are the professor who grades them.

Large research universities use subject pools that usually consist of the students in introductory psychology classes. Such systems can also be used at teaching institutions either by purchasing the services of an Internet-based subject pool company, or, if funding for that is not available, by using a bulletin board sign up method. In either case, the challenges are ethically motivating the students to participate and then managing the supply and demand of subjects and opportunities for the subjects to participate.

Finally, for research on learning and teaching methods, one possible tactic is to automate a study as much as possible on a Learning Management System (LMS). The challenge there is that, although the LMS probably has features that can be adapted for data gathering, they were not necessarily designed specifically for that purpose.

Subject Pools at Research Universities

In the social and behavioral sciences research is usually conducted using human subjects. Non-human animal subjects are also used sometimes, particularly in research on basic learning processes, but that is becoming less and less common. It is becoming increasingly expensive to house Non-human animals due to regulations about their care. Therefore, it is most likely that if you are going to conduct research in a discipline such as psychology, you are going to need human subjects.

In research universities it is typical for a psychology department to maintain a human subject pool. Such a pool usually consists of the undergraduate students in the introductory psychology classes, who are required, as part of the requirements for the course, to either participate in some number of hours of experience as human subjects, or to complete some kind of alternative assignment. Usually, the requirement is to earn some number of "credits," which is usually about 3 to 5. Usually, each credit is earned by participating in one hour's worth of volunteering or by doing one alternative assignment. The amount of credit earned per hour or per assignment can be something other than one hour, and the number of credits required can be whatever works well in a given situation. Also, as will be explained further below, those amounts can be part of the process of managing the supply and demand problem.

Those who need to run experiments using human subjects recruit from this pool. This enables the introductory psychology students to have the experience of being a human subject in order to help them to learn about research first hand, at least from the point of view of the subject. Such experience is considered a valuable educational experience for them as part of learning about the science of psychology. Of course, as will be explained further below, how educational it is depends in part on some of the details on how providing such an experience is actually carried out.

The researchers who will need subjects could be faculty members or research assistants working for the faculty members. Also, in some cases, undergraduate students in an experimental psychology course may be required to do research projects in which they will need to recruit human subjects from the subject pool. It could even be the case that undergraduate students in some other undergraduate courses, such as cognitive psychology, or a senior seminar, or a student doing independent research might be in that same position. At any rate, there needs to be a mechanism for those who need subjects to do the recruiting, and there needs to be a mechanism for the members of the subject pool to sign up to participate.

The mechanisms for recruiting and signing up could be direct recruiting from classes, posting the experiments for which subjects are needed on a bulletin board, or using a proprietary website. There is also now an open source website called OpenStax Tutor, which will be discussed further below, available for some situations. In the past, the bulletin board method was the most common at research universities. Now, however, the website method is much more common.

At an undergraduate teaching institution the situation could be different. Which recruiting and sign up method would be best could depend on such factors as the amount of funding available, how great the need is to conduct research, how many people need subjects, and how many subjects could be potentially available.

In some situations the need for human subjects might not be consistent across time. Even at a large research university where a lot of research is constantly being conducted, the need for, and the availability of, human subjects goes up and down somewhat during various times in a semester, and from semester to semester. At a small college or a community college, it might be the case that faculty or students do occasionally need human subjects, but exactly when that need occurs, and how many subjects are needed might be even more unpredictable than at a research university. In such cases it would be hard to set up a human subject pool system. One of the major challenges of such a system is to keep the supply and demand for subjects, and conversely, the supply and demand for opportunities to participate, in balance. That is not an easy task even at a large research university, and can be even more difficult at a small college.

Recruiting from Classes

When the need for human subjects is as unpredictable as it could be at a small college, then the best system might be to just directly recruit from classes. Doing so is different depending on whether you are recruiting from someone else's class or your own. Recruiting from your own class raises its own special problems. Therefore, I'll discuss recruiting from someone else's classes first, before discussing the special problems of recruiting from your own classes.

Recruiting from a Colleague's Class

Recruiting from someone else's class requires a good relationship between the faculty member doing the recruiting and the faculty member from whose class the subjects are recruited because it may be necessary to offer extra credit. In order to motivate the students to volunteer, there needs to be something in it for them. Of course, that raises the ethical issue of avoiding any incentive that could rise to the level of being coercive. To avoid any possibility of that question arising, and to avoid having to ask your colleague to offer extra credit in his or her class, the incentive could be just to do you a favor and to get some experience with research. Depending on how many subjects you need and how many students are in the classes from which you are recruiting, it is possible that that may be enough.

However, unless you need only a small enough number of subjects, perhaps 15 or 20, and you have a large enough number of students from which to recruit, perhaps 60 or so, you may need to offer more. There is also the issue that recruiting by just asking for a favor and touting the educational benefits of participating may result in a tendency for stronger or more motivated students to volunteer.

For many research questions that might not be an issue. However, you should be aware of that possibility in case that, due to the nature of your research question, it might be a real concern. If nothing else, it could raise the question of whether your results would generalize from the students who participated to students with a wider range of academic strength and motivation.

If you need a larger number of subjects relative to the size of the class from which you are recruiting, then you will probably have to offer more incentive to participate than just a request for a favor and the opportunity to learn first hand about research. If you have funding for your research you may be in a position to offer a cash payment. If the participation will require about an hour of the subject's time, and if you are offering the current minimum wage per hour, or even a little more, but not too much more, then that would probably not raise any question of being coercive. As a matter of fact, it might be necessary to offer a little more than the current minimum wage in order to be truly an incentive for the students, given that it is going to be a one-time participation and payment.

Motivating Students by Offering Extra Credit

It is more likely, however, that faculty at non-research universities will not have funding to pay subjects. Therefore, it is very common, when using the classroom recruitment method, to offer extra credit. Here, the question of coercion arises again, and it requires the cooperation of the teaching faculty member because your request now involves the structure of their class. Gaining the cooperation of a fellow faculty member for purposes of recruiting potential research subjects from their class, of course, requires the same kinds of social skills that should already be being applied to maintain good relations within a department. The best thing I can say here is to follow the age-old advice to treat the other faculty member the way you would wish to be treated. Be ready to try to put yourself in the other person's shoes, be willing to compromise, and be ready to offer to return the favor.

You should be aware of the size of the favor you are requesting. The need to ask a fellow faculty member to be willing to offer extra credit to their students involves more complications than you may initially realize. There is the ethical issue that all students must be treated equally. If a student has any qualms about volunteering to be a research subject, they still need to be offered the opportunity to earn the extra credit. Therefore, there needs to be some alternative method by which they can receive the extra credit. The alternative method of earning the extra credit must not be more burdensome than the research participation. Of course, these matters at some point come down to a judgment call, which will be made in cooperation with your Institutional Review Board (IRB), which is discussed further in Chapter 6. In any event, the teaching faculty member will need to keep track of the extra credits and include them in their grades. They also need to keep track of and to include in some way in their grades those students who do the alternative. Depending on exactly what you use as the alternative extra credit assignment, it may have to be graded as well. Whether any extra work for the class is done by the teaching faculty member or the researcher recruiting the subjects may be something that could be negotiated as part of the process of gaining cooperation. However, it is very tricky to suggest involving yourself in another faculty member's students' grades.

Recruiting from Your Own Classes

Recruiting from your own classes avoids the problem of asking for another faculty member's cooperation, but it raises its own ethical issues. Because the faculty member recruiting for the research is also the faculty member grading the students, there could be a conflict of interest. In order to avoid that conflict, your IRB will probably require that you use a procedure for recruiting the subjects by which you are not aware of which students volunteered and which did not until after you have determined the students' grades. A way to accomplish that would be for someone besides yourself to visit the class and go through the recruiting procedure while you are not in the classroom. I will have more to say about other aspects of good recruiting procedures below, but for my purposes here, I will explain how to recruit so as to avoid conflict of interest.

The person doing the recruiting, which could be a research assistant or a fellow faculty member, needs to give the recruitment speech and to pass out the informed consent forms. The informed consent forms should be given out with the instruction that the students should read the form, and then, if they decide they want to participate, they should sign and date the form, and, if not, they should leave it blank. Then all the forms should be collected. It is important to be clear that participation is only being requested and that participation is completely voluntary. You may think that it would be very obvious to both the person doing the recruiting, and to the students being recruited, that the students' permission is only being requested on a purely voluntary basis. However, from my experience it is very easy, especially if the recruiter is a research assistant, and that research assistant is in a hurry, which may very well be the case, for them to slip into just saying, "Please read this form and sign at the bottom." That implies that the students are being required to give their consent. And, as is explained further below, the undergraduate students may view the person doing the recruiting as an authority figure whom they should not question. At the time that the subjects are recruited, it is also important to make clear what, if any, incentive is being offered. If any incentive is being offered, then it is also important to make clear that the incentive can either be earned by volunteering or by doing the alternative.

When the informed consent forms are collected, they can be placed directly into an envelope by each student so that neither the recruiter nor any other student would know which students had agreed to participate. Using this procedure, it would be difficult for any student to know if any other student volunteered or not. And the faculty member teaching the course, who is also the researcher, would not know who volunteered.

The above procedure should satisfy the IRB that the recruitment of the subjects was done in a way that avoided conflict of interest. However, there is still the question of how the actual research procedure in which the data are gathered is to be performed while still avoiding conflict of interest. How that is done depends on the nature of the research method. It could be different depending on whether the recruitment procedure involved signing up to go to a lab at an appointed time to be run through the procedure versus participating right in the class during a future class time. In either event, if the data collection procedure would make the person collecting the data aware of which students had volunteered, then that person needs to be someone besides the faculty member teaching the class. Thus, given that the faculty member teaching the class is also the researcher, this is a case in which the researcher cannot collect the data themselves. That is not necessarily a problem, as long as it is possible for the researcher to train a research assistant to run the data collection procedure. That is, if the students have signed up to be run through the procedure at a later time, then the research assistant can run the subjects, and store the response sheets, or whatever medium is used to collect the data. Of course, this means that it might not be appropriate for the faculty member teaching the class to see the responses until after the grades for the class have been determined. If the responses contain no individually identifying information about the subject, then it may be acceptable for the faculty member to see the responses before the class grades have been determined. Still, there are other reasons for not peeking at the data before it has all been collected having to do with avoiding capitalizing on chance. Thus, it may be best for the faculty member not to see the responses until both all the data has been collected (which could take more than one semester) and all the grades for all of the classes involved have been determined.

However, what is to be done if it is not possible for the researcher to train a research assistant to run the data collection procedure? This could occur if the research involves comparing different teaching methods. That raises the problem that a research assistant cannot conduct the data gathering procedure. It is possible that such a problem could occur precisely because research on teaching methods is especially likely to be done at a teaching institution. Nevertheless, there may be a way around this difficulty.

Suppose that you intend to compare two teaching methods using the checkerboard design described in Chapter 3. In this situation, the data that you wish to collect is the students' performance on some classroom activity. Because the activity is part of the educational content of the class, all of the students perform the activity. It is not unethical to require all of the students to perform the activity because there are no potential risks to the subjects beyond what they would incur in their everyday life. At this point, the part of the everyday life we are referring to is participating in a college class. And the potential risk is the risk to their self-esteem if they find the classroom activity to be challenging. Such a risk cannot be avoided if one wished to obtain a college education.

On the other hand, you need the students' permission in order to use their performance on the activity as part of your data. This would be what they agreed to if they had agreed to participate at the time that the research assistant came to the class to recruit. As the faculty member teaching the class, you will have the records of the performance on the task from all of the students. However, the research assistant who collected the informed consent sheets has stored them away so that you do not know before determining the students' grades whose performance on the activities you will use as data. That will be determined after you have determined their course grades. You will do that by going through the consent sheets and only selecting for your data the performance of the students who gave their permission. Of course, once the data has been entered, and any information associated with the students' identities has been associated with the correct performance data, then an anonymous subject number will be associated with each subject and the names and any other individually identifying information will be stripped out of the data.

I need to point out, however, that a drawback to the method described above is that there remains the problem of students who miss class the day of the data collection activity. Given that it is not possible to have a research assistant hold a make up session and conduct the activity, then such a make up session needs to be provided by the faculty member. That may be a greater or a lesser problem depending on the nature of the data collection activity and the overall structure of the syllabus for the course. If it is a class that includes a lab, and if it is the case that not all potential lab sessions are typically used, then it may be possible to use one of the lab sessions that would otherwise not be used as the make up day for the data collection. If there is a grade attached to the activity, which is perfectly possible with such a procedure, that alone should be a fairly effective incentive to get the missing students to do the make up.

Subject Pools at a Teaching Institution

As described above, small colleges and four-year teaching universities are often in the position in which it would not be feasible to set up a subject pool. However, if the supply and demand of subjects for research and the supply and demand of opportunities for those subjects to participate in research is predictable enough, then it might be possible to set up a subject pool system even at such an institution. Bear in mind that the supply and demand issue will always be a problem that has to be managed. That even occurs at large research universities. Therefore, below I will discuss the various strategies for managing that problem.

Usually the students who form the subject pool are the students in the introductory psychology classes. That implies that there needs to be enough students taking introductory psychology to provide enough students to meet the researchers' demands for subjects. Also, typically, the means of motivating the students to participate in this situation is not extra credit. Instead, some amount of research participation is required as part of the requirements of the course. It may at first sound as if this is a violation of ethics. However, a closer look shows that it is not. There are two reasons for this. First, the students are given the opportunity to obtain their research participation either by signing up to be a subject in a study or by some other alternative means. Second, the usual benefits of research, which must outweigh the potential risks in order to allow the use of the subjects, are enhanced by the educational benefit to the students.

It is acceptable to have some research experience requirement as a requirement for a course. However, it would not be ethical if the only means to obtain that research experience were to volunteer to be a subject in a research study. If that were the case, then the participation would not really be voluntary because the need to succeed in a college course would be great enough to be considered coercive. However, if such volunteering were one possible way to meet the requirement, along with another alternative, then there may not be any problem of coercion. It is necessary, however, that the alternative method be no more burdensome for the student than being a subject. Typically, the alternative is to read a journal article about a research study, and to write a short summary of it in which the student must answer a few questions. The questions are designed so that answering them requires the student to demonstrate that they learned some of the same kinds of things that they would have learned had they participated in a study. For example, they could be asked to state the research question, identify the dependent and independent variables, describe the procedure used in the experimental and control conditions, and so on.

One question that may arise is whether a subject pool can be successful at providing the researchers with the subjects they need if students are allowed to meet their research experience requirement by doing the alternative. Fortunately, experience shows that the majority of students do volunteer to participate. This may be because they find the opportunity to do something that they have never done before appealing. Or it may be because, even though the alternative has satisfied the IRB that it is no more burdensome than participation as a subject, the students would still prefer to avoid it. At any rate, this method has been used successfully at many institutions for many years, and so you can be confident that it can work effectively.

Before discussing the second reason why subject pools can be run perfectly ethically, that is, because of their educational benefit, I will mention a possible concern related to the issue discussed in the previous paragraph. Just as students must be allowed an alternative way to meet their research experience requirement, they must also be allowed to withdraw from participating in a study even after they have given written informed consent and have begun their participation. They do not have to provide any reason for not continuing, and there can be no penalty for their withdrawal. The phrase "no penalty" is usually interpreted as meaning that they must be given their participation credit as if they had stayed for the full study.

The right of the subject to withdraw at any time without penalty may seem to raise the concern that students could take advantage of this right to earn all of their credits without actually fully participating in any study. My experience is that this concern is unfounded. I and my research assistants have run thousands of subjects over the years and I am not aware of a single time that a subject has withdrawn in such a way as to raise the suspicion that they were taking unfair advantage. Apparently, the social norm that once you agree to be a research subject you can't just walk out is strong enough to prevent such behavior. Apparently, as the classic Milgram (1963) experiments suggest, the experimenter represents to them an authority figure that they believe they cannot defy.

As a result, whenever one of my research assistants is acting as an experimenter, I instruct them to be aware of how the student volunteers might view them. I bring this point home by explaining that of the many subjects I have run, I have never had one appear to withdraw in an unfair manner. I add that if they were to instruct their subject to stand on one leg, jump up and down, and bark like a dog, the subject would probably just smile and obey. This emphasizes to them how important it is that they must be especially careful to be respectful and considerate toward their subjects.

Although I have never had a subject withdraw from a study in a way that suggested that they are taking unfair advantage, I have had the experience of a subject needing to leave during the procedure. However, the kind of dire circumstances that needed to arise to even make a subject legitimately exercise their right to withdraw should give you confidence that the right to withdraw does not pose any real problem for researchers. The only time I have ever had a subject leave during an experiment was one time when an adult subject received a cell phone call regarding something about her child that she needed to attend to right away. I also heard from one of my research assistants that they gave credit to one subject who had to leave due to becoming visibly ill during the study (not from anything that was done in the study; possibly from too much partying the night before).

The second reason why subject pools can be used ethically is because, in addition to whatever benefit to society there is from obtaining new knowledge, the subjects themselves benefit directly by the educational experience of participating in the study. Sometimes, especially in psychology research, the researcher needs to withhold some information about the study until after the subject has participated, because if the subject knew the information in advance, it might compromise the validity of the data. Sometimes it is even necessary to deceive the subject in some way. Typically, such withholding of information or deception is only about the hypothesis of the study. Because it is not about any potential risks that the subject would need to know about in advance in order for their consent to be truly informed, there is usually no ethical problem with the withholding of the information or even with the deception. Nevertheless, the subject has a right to know all about the experiment once their data has been collected. Thus, the researcher is required to provide the subject with a debriefing that informs them about the study. In the case of subjects from a subject pool, this debriefing also gives the researcher the means to provide the educational benefit. Thus, when students from a subject pool are used as participants, the debriefing should be written with providing that educational benefit in mind.

If undergraduate volunteer research assistants are being used as experimenters, then they usually require some special training in how to deliver the debriefing so as not to lose the educational benefit that it is supposed to provide. The experimenter needs to be aware of the importance of trying to maintain the subject's interest during the debriefing. The subject may feel that they have done their part to earn their credit, and now they just want to receive a pleasant "Thank you" and leave. Of course, there is also the matter of making sure that they have received their credit. Once the procedure for running the subject has been completed, the experimenter should thank the subject, and then they can say that they will give the subject their credit in a moment, but first, they will explain everything about the study in which the subject just participated. Doing so is one step in helping to motivate the subject to pay attention to the debriefing.

But there is another important step. That comes from the way the debriefing is provided. Typically, the debriefing is a one-page written description. As explained above, it should be as educationally valuable as possible. However, just handing the written debriefing to the subject before they leave risks the possibility that the subject will never read it. Instead, it should be read to the subject, and, partly to justify reading it instead of just handing it to them, the subject should be asked if they have any questions. Even though they seldom do, that should always be a part of the procedure.

Just as it is important to read the debriefing, it is even more important to read it so as to try to maintain the subject's attention. I have found that undergraduate research assistants almost always need some amount of training in order to develop the skill of reading the debriefing the way it needs to be read. I typically have a training session in which I first ask my research assistant to read a debriefing. They usually read it in a monotone, and much too quickly. I then give them an example of how to read it. I point out that the difference between their reading and mine is that I read much more slowly, I break each sentence into phrases, I emphasize particular words appropriately so as to enhance the meaning of what I'm reading, and I make frequent eye contact with the person to whom I am reading. Then I have them try it again. Typically, it takes a few such sessions to get them to read the debriefing as they should. I will even give them an example in which I somewhat exaggerate the pauses and emphases. I tell them that because they are unaccustomed to reading in this way, they may feel as if they are exaggerating when they are actually doing it just as they should. Some volunteers catch on to this quite quickly, others take quite a bit of training, but it is always important to get them well trained to do this for the sake of providing the full educational benefit to the subject. And it is beneficial to the research assistant as well to develop their communication skills in this way.

Methods of Implementing a Subject Pool

Before the Internet age subject pools were implemented by a bulletin board method. There are now companies that provide websites for managing a subject pool system for an annual fee. First, I'll describe how a bulletin board subject pool can be structured. In such a system you will need a centrally located bulletin board where researchers can post the studies for which they are recruiting subjects. There also needs to be a system to provide credit verification to the subject. Finally, someone has to administer the system.

Such a system can work well at an institution where the need to recruit subjects is somewhat consistent and predictable from semester to semester. The administrator needs to get information as far in advance as possible regarding how many researchers will be recruiting during a given semester and approximately how many subjects each researcher wishes to run. The administrator needs to know how much time is involved in participating in each study. Using this information, the administrator can get an idea of about how much demand there is going to be for subjects.

Then the administrator needs to get information regarding how many students are going to be available for the pool. Usually they come from the introductory psychology classes and they usually have some amount of participation requirement in terms of some number of credit hours. The administrator needs to know both the number of students and the number of required credit hours per student in order to know what the supply of subjects is going to be. The supply and demand can be referred to either from the researcher's perspective as the demand for subjects and their supply, or from the student's perspective as the demand for opportunities to participate and their supply. As I explain how a subject pool may be run, it is sometimes appropriate to refer to the supply and demand from one perspective and sometimes from the other. I'll try to make clear which way I'm referring to it each time I do so.

It should be clear from what I've said above that initiating a subject pool will require that all the faculty involved meet and discuss how they wish to do it. They will need to come to an agreement in advance because the success of the system depends on maximizing predictability. Also, I have said above that the subject pool usually comes from the introductory psychology classes. There can be times when a faculty member who teaches some other course may want to have a way to offer their students extra credit. In such cases, they may also want to use the subject pool. Once again, doing so will require the agreement and cooperation of all the faculty involved because problems will arise if you try to mix a subject pool that operates on a required credit system with using it for extra credit.

Once the administrator has an idea of what the supply and demand will be, it is possible to use this information to begin controlling them. Most of what is done to control supply and demand needs to be done before the semester starts. This is done by using the information described below, and by experience. If a problem with supply and demand becomes increasingly evident as a semester progresses, it is more difficult to manage that problem mid-stream. I will discuss below the possible methods of trying to manage such a problem, and the difficulties that arise.

In a smaller institution, this control function might be quite informal. It could even be the case that nothing special needs to be done. If the supply and demand are close enough to the same, then any difference can be accounted for by the students' ability to use the alternative option. That is, if the students are not finding quite enough opportunities to participate in order to meet their research credit requirement, then they can be reminded that the alternative is available. As long as not too many students need to use the alternative, and especially if they only need to do so for part of their requirement, the students may not mind doing so. However, you should be aware that if the students are having too much difficulty finding opportunities to participate, and as a result have to rely too much on doing the alternative, they may feel that the research requirement is unfair. Also, having the alternative available does not help if there are plenty of opportunities to participate and it is the researchers who are suffering from a shortage of supply of subjects.

In a larger institution there may need to be more formal ways to control supply and demand. I will first describe how this process may begin at a research university because at some teaching institutions the same tactic may be useful. I will begin by describing the process of crediting the subjects, and will then describe how rationing the credits can be used as a method to exercise some control over supply and demand.

If a bulletin board method of recruiting is being used, the credit may be granted by the researcher giving the subject a paper credit slip at the end of their participation. Typically, this slip is filled out to indicate what study the student participated in, the date and time, and it is signed by the experimenter. The student then turns in this credit slip to their professor to receive their research participation credit. One drawback to using this paper credit slip method is that the student has to be instructed that the credit slip is like cash. It has value, and if lost, is difficult to replace. You may wish to instruct students that if their credit slip is lost it cannot be replaced. Typically, however, students find such a requirement to be unfairly heavy handed. So, in practice, you may instruct them that if they lose their credit slip, then it is their responsibility to contact the experimenter who ran them through the procedure, and to plead with that experimenter to remember their participation and to contact their professor to verify the credit. However, that does not always go over very well with your research assistants who are running the subjects. Ultimately, there is no way for the crediting process to always run perfectly when you use paper credit slips. One way around this is to use some digital resource to handle the crediting, as will be explained below. But if this is not possible, then you will need to minimize problems as best you can. This can start with having the faculty who teach the introductory psychology sections that are providing the students for the subject pool give a stern warning that, although every effort will be made to make sure all the students receive their credits even if they lose their slip, having to do so will be met with disapproval and the burden of doing so will be considered to be mostly on the students themselves.

If a website method is used, you avoid some of the problems, such as lost credit slips, that can occur with the paper crediting method. However, such a website is more than just a recruiting tool. The many advantages of using such a website will be described further below. On the one hand, those advantages can make them very attractive, but, on the other hand, there is an annual fee for their use, whereas with the bulletin board method the only cost might be the initial purchase of a bulletin board, if one is not already available.

Once the administrator has collected the information about supply and demand described above, one possible way to begin exercising control is by rationing the credits. The number of subject hours that can be made available to all of the researchers for their studies is, strictly speaking, the number of students who are required to earn credits, times the number of hours each student is required to participate. The number of subject hours allotted to each research study could then be the total number of subject hours available divided by the number of research projects. That would assume, of course, that each project required the same number of subject hours and that there were no reasons to allot the subject hours differentially to different projects. One cannot expect those two assumption to hold. Therefore, some criteria as to how many subject hours will be allotted to each project will need to be agreed on. For example, the researchers may be allowed to not just ask that their study be included among those to which subjects will be allotted, but rather to request the number of subject hours they feel they will need. Also, there may be some hierarchy of precedence established. It might be that more senior faculty have precedence over more junior faculty or students. But it might also be, especially at a research university, that the graduate students have the highest precedence. At the University of Pittsburgh, where I did my graduate training, graduate students were generally given the highest precedence. But, factors such as how many times you had requested subject hours, the number of subject hours you requested, and whether you had previously used all of the subject hours that had been given to you were all taken into account as well. The ultimate goal is to strike the best balance possible between satisfying the needs of the researchers for subjects, and satisfying the needs of the students to meet their research requirement. It will require experience with running the system and ongoing negotiations to determine exactly how the subject hours are rationed.

The Structure of a Bulletin Board System

A researcher who wishes to recruit from the subject pool applies to the administrator for permission to use the pool. The administrator can make up a simple application form that asks the researcher for the information that is needed, including the information described above in the section on rationing credits. The administrator gives the researcher however many credit slips they are allotted. If there is a need to discourage counterfeiting the credit slips, that can be done by sequentially numbering all of the slips and maintaining a record of the slips each researcher received and gave out. Unused credit slips would then be returned to the administrator. It might happen that a researcher would need to request additional slips. Whether that would be allowed and how it would be handled would be one of the things that would need to be negotiated in advance of setting up the subject pool system.

Each researcher posts a flyer on the bulletin board describing their study and providing slots for the students to sign up to participate. The description of the study only needs to be brief. The student is not giving informed consent by signing up for the study. The informed consent will be requested when the student shows up for the appointment to be run through the procedure. It is usually the case that studies for which subjects are recruited in this way are very innocuous. However, there could be some things that it would be necessary to make clear in the description because the student would have to know them before deciding to sign up. For example, suppose there were requirements such as having normal vision without glasses or being left handed. Also, although it seldom happens, it is possible that there could be some risk for certain subjects. For example, suppose the procedure could possibly produce a high level of anxiety in subjects prone to anxiety. In cases such as those, the requirements or risks need to be made clear in the description.

It is unavoidable that the recruitment process will result in the researchers essentially competing for subjects. However, it is best to minimize that competition. The researchers should be required to write objective descriptions of their studies. They should be allowed to present their study in a way that minimizes the chance that it will appear less attractive to the potential subjects than the other studies, and they should be required to avoid efforts to make their study seem more attractive. For example, if their study involves a mathematical task, because many college students might tend to avoid that study, the researcher should be allowed to describe it simply as a problem solving task. On the other hand, researchers should not be allowed to describe their study as, for example, "fun" or "intriguing."

Before smart phones became as ubiquitous as they are today, the description and sign-up sheet would have tear-offs at the bottom with the essential appointment information, to serve as a reminder for the student. Such reminders may be less necessary today, given that students will probably have a smart phone with a calendar. However, if you are planning to use a paper bulletin board system, you may want to consider still having the researchers provide tear-offs. For one thing, there is no guarantee that all students would have a smart phone. Making that assumption might seem a bit discriminatory. Also, even if students have smart phones, there might be some tendency for them to neglect to put the appointment in their calendar. They might assume that they don't need to. Or they might plan to do it later and forget. Thus, seeing a tear-off might encourage them to be more responsible. Or, they might appreciate the convenience. For example, they might think that they will remember to put the appointment in their calendar later, but would appreciate having the tear-off with them as a backup.

The researchers need to monitor the bulletin board during the semester in which they are running their subjects. There is usually no need to encourage them to do so, given that it is to their advantage to stay on top of recruiting subjects. However, it might be the case that the description of the study is on one sheet, and the sign-up sheets are hung below. Then, it might be necessary to remind the researchers to take down their descriptions after the last subjects have been run.

Another consideration in running a subject pool system is that there must be rooms available for running subjects and access to those rooms needs to be managed. However, because that is essentially the same for a bulletin board system as for an Internet-based system, I'll discuss the many advantages of that type of system next. However, I'll begin by mentioning possible disadvantages.

An Internet-Based Subject Pool System

One possible disadvantage is that the Internet can go down whereas a bulletin board is always there. However, using a subject pool is only one aspect of students' lives that now rely on the availability of the Internet. The extent to which all of us have come to depend on the many advantages of having all sorts of resources available to us via the Internet apparently outweighs the inconvenience of the occasional Internet outage. For students, using an Internet-based subject pool is no doubt no exception.

The other disadvantage of such a system is its cost. However, the benefits of such a system may be well worth the cost. I'll describe them from the point of view of the product with which I have experience, Sona Systems. If your institution is interested in looking into using such a system, you will no doubt wish to look into the various products available and compare their costs and benefits for yourself.

The system allows anyone who has an email address at the institution that is paying for the system to create a user account. A user account can be for a participant, a researcher, a PI (principle investigator), an instructor, or an administrator. Participants are assigned an anonymous code number so that they can sign up for a study, participate, and receive their credit without the researcher ever seeing their name. In Sona Systems, a researcher and a PI have all the same functions within the system. The distinction is there in case a faculty member wishes to use research assistants, who may be undergraduate or graduate students, as experimenters to run subjects. The research assistants are designated as researchers, and the faculty member, who may or may not also act as one of the experimenters, but who is the supervisor of the research assistants, can have a separate designation as the PI. Instructors have to have user accounts because they go to the system to monitor their students earning of the research credits. Finally, an administrator has an account that gives them privileges to do anything on the system that they need to do.

I will not try to describe all of the features available on Internet-based subject pool systems for several reasons. First, the features might be different from one company to another. Also, features change over time. Finally, any system will provide up-to-date documentation which will provide all of the details of all of that system's features. However, I'll describe enough of the features of the system that I use, Sona Systems, to illustrate the many advantages of these types of systems in general, without necessarily advocating for any individual proprietary product in particular.

The researchers (which as explained above also includes the PI) can create a posting for their study by filling out a form. The form has fields for a title, a short description, and an optional longer description. It is also possible to place some requirements on who can participate and who cannot. Here is where the Internet-based method can do things that a bulletin board method cannot. If the requirements for participation are based on whether a potential subject has previously participated in some particular other study, then the system can enforce the restriction. The researcher sets the amount of time it takes to participate in the study, and they can also control how much lead time is needed to sign up for the study or to cancel.

The researcher can also designate a location, or several possible locations, where the study sessions will be run, and they can designate more than one person to be the researcher on the study. The researcher can then set the posting as active or inactive, and also as either visible to participants or not.

The researchers creates "time slots," that is, sessions in which some subjects will be run. The researcher can choose how many subjects to run and when to begin the session. The ending time of the session is set automatically based on the amount of time to participate that the researcher had set. It is also possible to either select a location from a drop down list, if several possible locations have been designated, or to write in a location. Finally, it is possible to designate which researcher, or researchers, will run that session, if more than one has been designated as being on the study.

This brings up the issue of locations for running studies. If more than one study is being run in any given semester, it may be necessary to either designate which researchers can use which locations, or at what times they can use them, or both. With a bulletin board subject pool, this might be accomplished either by some advance arrangement, or by putting sign up sheets on doors at the various locations. With an Internet-based subject pool system, some advance arrangement might also be necessary. However, the Internet-based system may have the feature of preventing double bookings of locations, or at least the feature of an alert that a double booking had taken place.

The students in the subject pool can be instructed to go to the website for the Internet-based subject pool system and to create their participant accounts, or the system may allow the instructor to enroll all of his or her students as a batch. It is important for the students to receive adequate instructions in what is expected of them in regard to their research experience requirement, and how to meet the requirement. You must keep in mind that the students will probably have some misconceptions about what participating in research as a subject means. They may think, for example, that it means filling out a survey form. They may not realize that many studies present tasks for the subject to perform that can be any of a variety of things. They may have some apprehension about being a subject. They may suspect that they are going to be subjected to some embarrassing or otherwise aversive experience. And they often assume that they will be deceived about the purpose of the experiment. Therefore, part of the instructions should include reassuring the students that the researchers will follow established procedures to treat them respectfully, as well as about all of their rights, and all of the other ethical requirements that the researchers must follow. With an Internet-based system, they will probably be presented with, and required to verify that they have read, a document advising them of their rights as a subject and the ethical responsibilities of the researchers.

Beyond making sure that the students know about the true nature of participating in research, it is also necessary to emphasize to them very strongly how important it is for them to be responsible about keeping their appointment. It might be a good idea to have the subject pool administrator visit the classes at the beginning of the semester to make sure the students have been told these things. That can also be an opportunity to demonstrate the use of the subject pool website.

Once the students are ready to participate, and once a study has been created, made active and visible, the participants can view the description of the study in the same way that they would be able to go to a physical bulletin board and read the descriptions posted there. For each study, they will see whether it has time slots. If there are any available, the student can easily sign up for one of them with a click of the mouse. A problem can arise, however, if students have trouble finding enough available time slots to meet their requirement. Similarly, it is a problem for the researchers if there are not enough students signing up for studies. Planning ahead, and possibly using a credit rationing system, as discussed above, are done to avoid running into either of these supply and demand problems mid-stream. In a separate section below, I will discuss the measures that might be considered if such a problem does arise.

Once students have signed up for a time-slot, there is the possibility that they might need to cancel. One important advantage of an Internet-based system is that it makes it easy for students to do so. They simply go back to the time-slot and with another click of the mouse they cancel, thus opening up that slot for other students. Unfortunately, despite the ease of such a cancellation, some students will fail to do so, or they will discover their need to cancel after the deadline for cancellation has passed. Thus, there will always be some amount of no-shows for appointments.

An Internet-based system may allow you to keep track of such no-shows. However, it is very important to know that the United States Office for Human Research Protections (OHRP—part of the U.S. Department of Health and Human Services) has ruled that studies that receive U.S. federal funding, or studies at a university that has a Federal Wide Assurance (FWA) in place cannot impose a penalty for no-shows. They treat it the same as penalizing a subject for withdrawing after agreeing to participate in a study. Also, many university IRBs will apply the same ruling to all the studies conducted at their university unless they are so innocuous as to be ruled exempt from IRB oversight. Researchers should consult with their own institution's IRB for advice on this matter. The important thing to know, however, is that in any case where this ruling applies you cannot, for example, increase the amount of research experience required as a penalty for a no-show. At the same time, if there is no way to discourage no-shows, experience shows that the no-show rate could be 2 to 3 times higher than if there is some way to discourage them. Fortunately, there are two things that you are allowed to do to discourage no-shows.

To discourage no-shows, first, if a student has some number of no-shows you can limit the amount of credit that the student is allowed to earn by actually participating as a subject, and instead, require them to earn the balance of their required credits by doing the alternative. Second, you can give some sort of bonus to students who have incurred no, or few, no shows.

Another major advantage of an Internet-based system is that once the subject arrives at their appointment and the experimenter has run them through the procedure, their credit is granted on the subject pool website. This requires having Internet access at the location where the subject is run, which is usually not a problem because Internet connected computers are now so ubiquitous. In addition, your research assistant will probably be carrying a smart phone with Internet access. The subjects are identified to the researcher on the website only by an anonymous code number. As long as all of the subjects for a time-slot show up, the experimenter simply credits all of the numbers for that time-slot. Thus, there would not even be a problem of one or more of the students did not know their assigned code. The students all leave the session confident that they have received their credit, and there is no slip to be turned in, which, as discussed above in the section on bulletin board systems, could be lost. If there is a no-show, however, it would be a slight problem if one or more students did not know their code number. If that happens, it can still be dealt with very easily. The subject who needs to find his or her code can simply log on to the subject pool website on the computer in the room or on his or her smart phone and check his or her profile to find the code number.

Another important advantage of an Internet-based subject pool system is that the instructors for the courses providing the students for the pool can simply go to the subject pool website to see the credits the students have earned. So, as you can see, an Internet-based system facilitates the whole process from posting studies, to sign ups, to crediting the subjects.

An Internet-based subject pool system will also provide many reports that can be very helpful for building up experience useful for managing the difficult task of controlling supply and demand. They are too numerous and complex to be detailed here, but any Internet-based subject pool provider will have documentation to which to refer. Two other important and related tasks will be end of semester maintenance and setting up the subject pool at the beginning of the next semester. However, again, your provider will no doubt have documentation to help with these tasks.

At my institution, when I first started managing our subject pool system, I found that, as it grew, the demands on my time to run it were becoming quite high, given my teaching load and expectations for service to my department and the university. This occurred largely because we eventually began making our subject pool available for our experimental psychology students to recruit from for their class projects. Fortunately, we have had a steady stream of excellent graduate assistants in our department to whom we have been able to delegate most of the work of running the subject pool. These graduate assistants have learned to do the end of semester maintenance, the beginning of the semester instructions to the introductory psychology students who make up the pool, the beginning of the semester talks to the experimental psychology students to instruct them in and to demonstrate the use of the pool, and much of the day-to-day work. It should be comforting to know that it doesn't take an advanced degree to run such a system. It just requires a competent, organized person who can read and understand the documentation and who is diligent enough to stay on top of the tasks.

Here are some of the day-to-day tasks that have come up in the process of running our subject pool. Each time a researcher creates a posting of an experiment to go on the subject pool website it has to be approved by an administrator. This is not the same as IRB approval. Faculty and students working under the supervision of a faculty member need to know to get IRB approval first. Your Internet-based system may provide a place to enter an approval code from the IRB to verify to subjects that the study has that approval. However, the administrator has the opportunity to look at the description of the study to be sure it meets the noncompetitiveness requirements described earlier. They may also check to make sure that the amount of credit being given for the study looks like it meets the agreed on amount of credit for the amount of time the study will take.

At our institution in addition to the faculty in our department using our subject pool, we also allow the experimental psychology students to do so. Typically, a faculty member will post a study in one semester, but continue it for as many semesters as needed to gather the amount of data they wish to gather, whereas the experimental psychology projects are only for one semester. Therefore, when doing the end of semester maintenance it is very helpful for the administrator to have a quick and easy way to distinguish the experimental psychology projects just from their title, so that they can be removed without the need for further checking. Our graduate assistants came up with the solution of having all of the experimental psychology projects being required to have a title that ended with "Fall 2015," or whatever semester they were run in. Thus, when the administrator receives a request for a posting, among the things they check is to see if the study is a one-semester student project, and, if so, if it is titled as required.

Among the various little day-to-day things that may come up with the administration of the subject pool, a couple of others deserve mention. Sometimes a subject will need to cancel an appointment at the last minute. Sometimes a subject may have already missed an appointment. Or sometimes a subject may have shown up at the time and place that they believed they were supposed to show up, only to find no experimenter there. In any of those cases, the subject believes that they should not be deprived of their credit. Those cases require a little investigation to determine whether the reason for the last minute cancellation or missed appointment can be considered legitimate. Or, in the last case, some investigation is required to determine whether a researcher really failed to show up, or the subject went to the wrong place or at the wrong time. What is required is not only investigation but the application of some good judgment. In my experience, the best policy is to appear to be very serious about collecting all of the information, but then to be reasonably lenient in allowing the student to receive his or her credit. That is how I have instructed the graduate assistants who serve as co-administrators of my subject pool system, and I know of no serious problems that have resulted.

There is one more very important point before leaving the topic of the day-to-day administration of the subject pool. Successful and smooth operation of the system benefits from experience. If it seems more difficult than you had anticipated at the beginning, you can be confident that with time and experience you can make it get easier. But, very importantly, if you are using graduate assistants to help you, do not forget to account for the fact that they will learn a lot from their experience, but then they will move on. There must be a deliberate method to maintain the institutional memory. If you are lucky enough to have more than one graduate assistant, and the more senior ones overlap with new ones as the most senior ones leave, then the task of passing on the knowledge and experience of running the subject pool will be easier. However, even in such a case, it is important to impress on the graduate students who gain the experience that you need them to pass it on to a junior colleague so that you are not left in the lurch when they leave. If you only have one graduate assistant at a time, it will be more difficult. Nevertheless, anything that you can do to encourage whoever helps you with the subject pool to document the various problems that occur, the various solutions that were tried, and how well they worked will be invaluable later.

Managing Supply and Demand Mid-Stream

As mentioned above, the major task with any subject pool system is managing supply and demand, and the most important part of that process is your advance planning. Nevertheless, as a semester progresses either the students can begin complaining that they can't find enough opportunities to participate, or the researchers can begin complaining that they are not getting enough subjects.

Regarding the supply of subjects: it is usually greater in a fall semester than in a spring semester. Also, at the beginning of a semester there is usually a surge of conscientious students who are looking for opportunities to participate in order to get their research experience requirement out of the way as soon as possible. After about the middle of the semester there is usually a drop off of students signing up. Then, at the end of the semester, there is usually another surge of less conscientious students trying to sign up because they have left meeting their research experience requirement until the last minute.

Regarding the demand for subjects: from faculty researchers it is likely to be no different in the spring semester than in the fall. The faculty researchers may prefer to have the more conscientious students who sign up at the beginning of the semester as subjects in their studies, especially if their study calls for serious task involvement. Any student researchers, especially if they are students recruiting for an experimental psychology class project, will not be recruiting until the end of the semester.

Part of the correspondence between the timing for the supply and demand may seem fortuitous. That is, the faculty researchers are more likely to benefit from the early sign up of the conscientious students than the student researchers. Not to disparage the student researchers, but their projects are for a learning experience, not necessarily for publication. Therefore, it is of less consequence to them if their subjects are the less conscientious ones. Nevertheless, some faculty projects may not be particularly dependent on task involvement, but may require a large number of subjects, and so the wealth of conscientious subjects at the beginning of the semester may not be particularly beneficial to them, whereas the drop off in the middle might hurt them. Also, in my experience, the surge of subjects at the end of the semester comes late enough so that even though the experimental psychology students do not post their studies until somewhat later in the semester, they are still sometimes plagued by a lack of subjects. As a result, no matter how much planning you try to do in order to ration out the subjects effectively to the researchers, there can still be problems that occur mid-stream.

Once the semester is in progress, there may be some things that you can do to affect the supply and demand, but they are not always as effective as you would like, and some have to be used very carefully, if at all. If subjects are not getting enough opportunities to participate, one thing you can try is to come up with a study, any study, that is simple, and can be posted quickly enough to be helpful. For that purpose, it might be helpful for the administrator to have in mind some quick and easy study, perhaps a survey, that they can have at the ready should it be needed. You could also appeal to your fellow faculty members to do the same. It can even be a study that is not intended to produce any publishable data. As long as it can be available to absorb some of the demand for opportunities to participate it will have served its purpose. And there is nothing to say that it could not also serve some other purpose. It might be something that could be especially educational for the subjects. It might be something the data from which you could use as a teaching tool in a later experimental or statistics class. It might even be an attempt to replicate a study already in the literature, something whose importance is becoming more greatly appreciated in the field recently. Notice, however, that this is a measure that, although it might be possible to implement at a moment's notice, would be much better if planned for in advance. One thing that makes a dearth of opportunities to participate less problematic than a dearth of subjects is that the subject pool students can always, even if only as a last resort, be steered to the alternative.

The problem of the researchers not getting enough subjects is more difficult. One thing you can try is to appeal to the instructors of courses other than the introductory psychology classes to have their students available for the subject pool. But there are several problems. The subjects in the other classes may have already participated in the subject pool in an earlier semester. Because of their earlier participation, and because of the courses that they may have taken, they may not be at the same level of naivety to the hypotheses being investigated as the introductory psychology students. Another problem is how to motivate them to sign up. If there is only a request to do so, you may not get enough response to be helpful. If you give them extra credit, then their motivation to participate is different from that of the introductory psychology students. Either of these factors might not be a problem for some types of studies, but it may be for others. Finally, there is the problem that you would be asking a fellow faculty member to change the structure of their course after the syllabus has already been given to the students.

There is one other way to try to increase the number of participants, but it is especially problematic. Let's say that you had determined that the studies for the semester lasted anywhere from about 5 minutes up to about 90 minutes. You decided initially that you would advertise that each hour of participation would be worth one credit. But, in order to be a little bit generous to the subjects, you had given the researchers the guideline that any study lasting only up to 19 minutes would be worth 1/2 credit, and any study from 20 minutes up to 49 minutes would be one credit. Any study from 50 minutes to 79 minutes would 1 1/2 credits, and any study from 80 minutes to 109 minutes would be worth 2 credits.

If you find mid-stream that you need more subjects, then here is what you could do. You know that the experimental psychology students have yet to post their studies, and that their studies are often of short duration. You could require that any study lasting only up to 14 minutes would be worth 1/4 credit. Then, in that same fashion, students would be given 1/4 credit for each 15 minutes of participation. That would not be a change from one credit per hour, as originally advertised. But it would slice up the hour into smaller pieces and enable the researchers to give smaller pieces of credit. If you knew that many of the experimental psychology students' projects would be less than 14 minutes long, you would be giving out many 1/4 credits. And a 15 minute to 39 minute study would now cost you only 1/2 credit instead of a whole credit. Thus, the subject pool subjects would have to participate in more studies to earn their required credits, effectively increasing the number of credit hours available. But there is the problem of basic fairness of having treated earlier signing up students differently than later ones, and without their expecting the change. Perhaps a justification for doing this would be that you did not deviate from what you advertised, that the students would not even have experienced the change had they been more conscientious and signed up earlier, and that you made the change for a good purpose. Let your conscience be your guide.

Given that Internet-based subject pool systems have all of the advantages described above, but that they are proprietary and must be paid for, you might be tempted to think about either looking for an open source version or using whatever computer science talent you have at your institution to build your own system, rather than paying for a proprietary system. Generally speaking, I am very supportive of open source software. I have found much of it to be of excellent quality, easy to use, and easy to find support for. However, at the time of writing this I know of no open source subject pool system, although it is possible that there is one out there that I have not found, or that may be developed at some time in the future.

Regarding trying to build your own in-house system, I have received advice against trying to do that. On the one hand, the advice comes from Sona Systems, the proprietary system that we use at my institution, and so you might wish to take into consideration that it is in their interest to provide such negative advice. On the other hand, I can report that I have had a very good experience with that company and have a very good relationship with them. At any rate they have given me permission to share this advice, and you can evaluate it for yourself. They gave the following reasons not to try to build your own subject pool system:

- The person who wrote it graduated and no one knows how it works.
- It runs on the university's servers in their main datacenter, but it isn't a priority in the IT department to keep it maintained. We saw this when the

university's main email system went down right at the end of the semester. That took priority over fixing the subject pool system server, so grades were delayed.

- It doesn't run on the university's main servers, but rather on a computer in the department. That computer or the facilities aren't maintained (like one case where they had it in the basement and the basement flooded).

- The software isn't written with full understanding of the human subjects regulations and privacy issues.

- The software isn't written with an eye toward data security. Hacking is big business now, so software needs to be written carefully to prevent security breaches, and the underlying servers need to be maintained accordingly. Both these take a certain level of expertise that a grad student may not have.

- Support. What if the person who wrote it is out sick, busy with other tasks, etc.? Often they get busiest at the end of the semester, when timing for the pool is also critical to get grades in.

- Costs are overlooked. In-house programmers aren't entirely "free" and even at $10 an hour, it's a lot cheaper just to pay for our software.

You can make of that advice what you will, but I will point out that they made several points that I would not have thought of.

Conducting Research on Learning and Teaching Methods on an LMS

Many institutions now use Learning Management Systems (LMSs) as a resource for their instructors and students. Given that research on learning and teaching methods is a natural fit for a teaching institution, it is also natural to consider using the LMS as a mechanism to collect data. One possible way to do this is to use the LMS's facility for presenting tests or homework activities as a way to present tasks and their associated stimulus materials to students after asking them to give their informed consent to allow their performance on the tasks to be used as data in a study. In Chapter 3, I had briefly mentioned my experience with collecting data in this way. In that study, I manipulated two factors together and examined their impact on learning some basic concepts in statistics. The concepts that the students were trying to learn were which statistical procedure to use to analyze the data from a particular study, given a description of the research question and the methodology of the study. The first factor that was manipulated was whether, in the experimental condition, the students practiced retrieving the information that they studied, or, in a control condition, they merely saw the information presented a second time. The second factor that was manipulated was that in the experimental condition, along with practicing retrieval, the subjects did their two study sessions with a gap of two weeks between them whereas, in the control condition, along with just seeing the information a second time instead of practicing retrieving it, their two study sessions were separated by a gap of only one day. We tested the subjects immediately after their last study session, and again 11 weeks later at the end of the semester. Our primary hypothesis was that the experimental subjects should perform better than the control subjects at retaining the association between a particular type of research design and the appropriate statistical procedure for analyzing the data from that design.

The first part of the manipulation, practicing retrieval, worked well using this method. It turns out that implementing the second part, the length of the gap between study sessions, was complicated by a rather large number of students not doing the homework assignments when scheduled. A possible way to improve on such a study would be to have a large enough group of subjects participating so that, even with some students being less than fully diligent in their compliance, there would be enough subjects who did comply to give the study high statistical power. Examining the data from the study we conducted on our LMS is still ongoing at this writing. However, a quick preliminary look shows that the manipulation may have supported the primary hypothesis.

Using an LMS to automate the study described above was useful, even though the LMS was not particularly designed for conducting research. This led me to do an Internet search to see if I could find a resource that was like an LMS, or at least that could be used as a resource for students, but also could be a resource for the teacher to conduct research on learning. I found an initiative of Rice University called OpenStax. Although it is not an LMS, it provides some useful open source resources for students. Furthermore, the developers of the site base its features on empirical research that they conduct, and instructors can help with that research.

OpenStax provides free open source textbooks on a variety of subjects (https://openstaxcollege.org/books) and they are developing courseware called OpenStax Tutor, which is still under development at this writing. The courseware that OpenStax Tutor is developing is software that is similar to software that companies develop to target advertising to potential customers based on things like their Internet surfing and buying behaviors. OpenStax Tutor is developing similar software to target the best possible learning experiences to a student, based on things like their performance on tests and homework, and on behaviors such as which examples they chose to look at and for how long. The courseware is designed to enhance the use of the textbooks by guiding the student toward a personalized experience.

Using the older OpenStax Tutor system (www.openstaxtutor.org), instructors could set up a course and use one of the textbooks that was enhanced with the courseware. OpenStax would use the students' performance as they used the courseware as data for further development. Thus, an instructor was helping OpenStax Tutor to advance educational research just by using the system. The OpenStax Tutor research team determined the research questions to be asked, but instructors were considered to be collaborators in the research. That older system is being deprecated and the new version is still being developed and is not yet available to the public. However, if an instructor wished to use OpenStax Tutor as a resource to help them in their own research, their head research scientist, Philip Gimaldi, Ph.D. says, "We are absolutely open to the idea of working with instructors/researchers on their own research questions, provided those questions fit with our general research agenda" (personal communication, 01/07/16). To learn more about the possibility of doing so, one would have to contact Dr. Grimaldi at phillip.grimaldi@rice.edu.

Summary

To recruit human subjects from a colleague's class requires tactful negotiation of issues such as asking the colleague to offer extra credit and an alternative participation method. To recruit subjects from one's own classes will require a method of avoiding the inherent conflict of interest created by the researcher also teaching and grading the class. This could involve, for example, using graduate assistants or colleagues to carry out the recruitment process.

Any subject pool system, whether a bulletin board sign up system or an Internet-based system requires managing the supply and demand of subjects and opportunities for the subjects to participate. That management requires gathering information at the beginning of the semester, monitoring the system during the semester, and applying the experience gained each semester to plan the next one. Supply of opportunities to participate can be aided by having some easy to implement studies waiting in the wings should they be needed. The supply of subjects can be tweaked by adding extra classes to the pool, but that will entail some of the same challenges as recruiting from classes.

Finally, for research on learning and teaching methods it is sometimes possible to implement a study on an LMS. For example, stimulus material can be presented as enrichment content and data can be gathered by online quizzes. For maximum flexibility in using an LMS for data gathering, however, what is needed is an LMS that is specifically designed to serve as a research platform.

Suggested Readings

https://www.sona-systems.com/ Sona Systems

> This company provides an Internet-based subject pool system for managing all aspects of gathering data from human subjects. Among the facilities it provides are the ability to conduct both experimental and survey research, automatic screening of subjects based on previous participation, and many useful reports to help manage supply and demand.

https://openstaxtutor.org/ OpenStax Tutor

> From this site you may be able to learn about the history and some of the development of this initiative. However, according to its developers, this site may not continue to be available.

https://tutor.openstax.org/ OpenStax Tutor

From this site you may be able to see more about where this initiative is headed. However, according to its developers it is still in beta testing.

Reference

Milgram, S. (1963). Behavioral study of obedience. *The Journal of Abnormal and Social Psychology, 67*(4), 371–378.

5
RECRUITING UNDERGRADUATE VOLUNTEER RESEARCHERS

After Reading This Chapter You Will Know How to

- Appreciate the advantages of having undergraduate research students
- Recruit undergraduate volunteer research assistants
- Select the most promising undergraduate research assistants
- Motivate and manage research assistants
- Coordinate conference submissions and attendance with research assistance

Introduction

One of the most significant factors that can make or break your ability to conduct meaningful research at your institution is your ability to recruit committed research assistants. Although it may take some time to identify and train qualified students, once they are engaged in your program they can work on almost all aspects of your research. This assistance will free up your schedule allowing you to balance your teaching and research activities. Having student assistants will also allow you more time to focus on the aspects of the research that only you can accomplish.

The current chapter discusses some of the advantages of having undergraduate students as research assistants, highlights some student recruitment and selection strategies, examines how to motivate and manage research assistants, and discusses issues relating to taking students to research conferences.

The Advantages of Undergraduate Students

Although you may think that being at a teaching institution with smaller numbers of graduate students, if at all, limits your ability to attract good students to assist with your research, the truth is that when approached correctly, the potential of drawing great students to help with your research at teaching institutions is remarkable.

There are two significant factors that work in your favor. First, since as a teaching institution your department probably does not have many traditional graduate students, you have to rely on undergraduate students for help with research projects. This can serve as a significant advantage which research institutions do not provide. In traditional research institutions the abundance of graduate students limits the opportunities for undergraduate students to be involved in research. In many ways undergraduate student assistants are more valuable than graduate assistants. First, many undergraduate students want to get into graduate school. The incentive of the benefit of research experience for graduate school admission is powerful and must be emphasized to the student. This desire can serve as a powerful motivator for undergraduate students as they work on your research work.

Additionally, very often, undergraduate students have fewer responsibilities than graduate students and thus are more available to commit themselves to the research work. They probably live on campus as well and hence are more inclined to work during odd hours, which is when most research at a teaching institution is conducted anyway.

The second benefit that works in your favor at a teaching institution is that you may be one of the few faculty members in your department conducting real student-based research and consequently the number of students available to assist with your project may be considerable.

Hence, when approached correctly, the possibilities inherent in the area of utilizing undergraduate research assistants can be extremely beneficial and thus require some direction in all steps of the process.

Recruiting Undergraduate Volunteer Research Assistants

In order to truly recruit the students you need for your project, the recruitment process must be looked at from "outside the box." Your recruitment efforts must take on a multifaceted approach. There are primarily three avenues to pursue in your recruitment efforts: classroom publicity, campus-wide publicity, and word of mouth/online publicity.

Classroom Publicity

The most salient benefit of classroom publicity is that it offers the opportunity of getting the word out to many students at one shot and provides legitimacy to your project in the eyes of the students. All you need is five willing colleagues to allow you to come into their classrooms for just a few minutes and without much effort you have an audience of several hundred students. When you present your "job talk" to the students there are several essential pieces of information that should be included: a brief description of the project, the benefit for the students in joining, and how they can contact you. The description should be limited to a paragraph or two about the general objective of the project without getting too specific. Spend most of the time talking about the benefits to the students in joining the project such as career objective clarification, graduate school admission, and resume enhancement.

An additional benefit that draws the students attention is the conferences you plan on submitting your work to and the possibility of traveling to exotic places to attend these conferences. Your institution may even have funding for undergraduates to attend conferences, which should be mentioned as well.

End your presentation with an easy way in which the students can contact you. You want this presentation to be short, which is why more detailed information, such as time commitment by the students, tasks that will be required by the students, or a description of the method of data analysis that you plan on utilizing should all be eliminated and clarified to the students later on once they approach you individually with interest. Don't be concerned about selecting the good students now; cast as wide a net as possible at this point. Selecting the students that will be most beneficial to you comes later. At this point you just want to get the word out and have as many students as possible approach you so you have a large pool of applicants to choose from.

Campus-Wide Publicity

The second avenue to pursue in your recruitment efforts is campus-wide publicity. In order to access the most students possible, your recruitment efforts should take on the characteristics of a publicity campaign for a student club party. A campus-wide flyer campaign, targeting the high traffic areas of the campus using a flashy flyer, may be your best option. As you can tell from the sample flyer (Figure 5.1), it should not include a detailed elaboration on the project; students are less likely to read flyers with lots of words on them. A brief overview of the study, benefits for the student, and contact information is all that need be included.

Research opportunity!
Students are needed to assist in a developing research study on the sibling relationships of high school students

❒ Gain hands-on experience to enhance your applications for graduate school or employment.
❒ Independent research credits and funding may be available to qualified students.
❒ Opportunity to co-author papers based on the project and attend national conferences.

For more information contact:
Dr. A. Milevsky
Psychology Department, OM 390
(610) 683-1363
Milevsky@Kutztown.edu,
faculty.kutztown.edu/milevsky

FIGURE 5.1 Sample flyer.

In order to identify the high traffic areas on campus, you may want to get a copy of a campus map and mark on the map the areas that fit into the following two categories: congregating areas and high movement areas. Congregating areas are areas on campus which serve as a hang out area for the students such as the food court area or areas with places to sit around. You may also find several congregating areas on campus right outside large classrooms where students stand around when waiting for their next class. A second target area is what is called "high movement areas" which are several key intersections on campus that experience high movement between classes. Simple campus observation will reveal these places on campus, or you can identify on the map the largest classroom buildings on campus and draw lines on your map between these buildings and then highlight the areas on your map that have the most intersection of lines. Once you have identified these two high traffic areas on campus, post as many flyers as you can in these areas.

There are several other tools at your disposal to enhance your campus-wide publicity. Again, thinking of these efforts in terms of a publicity campaign for a fraternity house party can be extremely beneficial. Campus-wide email announcements, student newspapers, daily bulletins, and the university radio station can all be utilized. A quick call to your university's public relations office can connect you with the appropriate people to help you in these endeavors.

Word of Mouth/Online Publicity

The third avenue to pursue in your recruitment efforts is word of mouth and online publicity. Word of mouth is extremely beneficial once you already have a few committed students who are willing to get the word out. Have them mention your research work to some of their friends and classmates. Once the ball is rolling, word of mouth publicity takes on a life of its own and may prove to be your best method of recruitment.

You can also establish a Facebook page or Twitter account for your research. Increasingly, the current cohorts of students are utilizing these avenues for things that go beyond interpersonal connections. You can have a link to these accounts set up directly from your department's website. Once you have recruited the initial group of students you can have them link to your Facebook or Twitter pages. You may also be able to delegate this online recruitment task to one of your research students as we will discuss shortly.

Other Recruitment Considerations

An additional consideration that must be examined regardless of the method of recruitment you employ is who your target student is. If you are working on a longitudinal project or on a project that requires extensive training, you may want to look for younger students (i.e., freshman or sophomores) to join your project. The earlier you get them the more involved they will become and you may have some great students working with you for several years. If indeed you determine that you will benefit most from students in the first few years of their under-graduate education, your publicity should be focused on classes and areas around campus that cater to these students. If you pursue classroom publicity, your focus should be on general education classes which enroll mostly freshman and sopho-more students. Some of the general classes that are taught in large classrooms fall into this category. There are also areas around campus that are notorious for attracting underclassman. Ask any aware junior or senior student about the areas on campus that attract freshman and sophomore students and their response can provide the information you need.

On the other hand, if you are not looking for student assistance longevity or if the tasks you plan on assigning the students require knowledge of statistical procedure, for example, you may be in need of more advanced students and may want to target more advanced classes for your classroom presentations.

Another recruitment aspect to consider is that your target students may not necessarily be students in your major; there are many other disciplines that may be related to your work and students from those disciplines may be interested in joining your project. For example, research in psychology may be of interest to counseling students, social work students, sociology students, education students, or even criminal justice students. Hence, publicizing your project exclusively in your department or in your department's classes may limit your prospects.

Selecting Undergraduate Volunteer Research Assistants

Once you have a steady stream of students contacting you for more information about your project, you can begin providing more detailed information to the students about your work and you can start the process of selection. Aside from elaborating on the project, make sure to be as specific as possible about what aspects of the project the students will be involved in and about the actual tasks the students will be required to complete. For most of these students this may be the first time they are involved in any research project, the idea of which may be extremely overwhelming for them. Detailing the tasks that may be required from them may help in alleviating their concerns. Try to provide the students with an estimate of the time commitment involved in joining the project.

After the initial meetings with students who have expressed interest in joining your project, it is time to consider selecting the right students. There are primarily two approaches that you can follow based on the nature of your project and the tasks you plan on assigning to your students.

The "Exclusive Club" Model

The first approach, which is appropriate for studies that necessitate extensive training, is the model we like to call the "exclusive club" model. In this approach, you apply a rigorous selection and admission process to your project in order to guarantee that the students joining your project are committed, will truly contribute to the study, and have the drive and willingness to follow through on assignments. If you choose this approach, your initial contact with an inquiring student should include handing them an application and setting up a time for an official interview. As you can see in Figure 5.2, the application should include questions about some basic work and research background and should include space for references.

Have the students drop off the application at your office or in your department mailbox as soon as possible so you have time to review and check references before the interview. The speed at which the application is returned to you can serve as an additional gauge of the student's professionalism, enthusiasm, and competence. The interview does not have to be long but should have an interview feel to it. The questions you ask during the interview can serve as a follow up to the questions on the application. This process will help you in selecting the most qualified students and will convey to the students the importance of the work and the privilege of working on the project if selected.

Your selection process should generate three tiers of students; the best, the possible, and the rejected. Begin by reaching out to the students you are most interested in and invite them to an initial group project meeting. It may happen that even after this process you may hear back from a selected student that their schedule changed and they are no longer interested in working on the project.

RESEARCH ASSISTANT APPLICATION FORM

NAME _____ E-MAIL _____

PHONE #1 _____ PHONE #2 _____

ADDRESS _____

MAJOR _____ YEAR: Fr So Jr Sr Grad CURRENT GPA _____

Are you employed outside of school? __ No __Yes No. Hrs/week _____

If employed, what type of job do you have? _____

How many credit hours are you taking this term? _____

Previous employment experience:

School activities (past or present):

Volunteer activities (past or present):

Any other experience that might be helpful?

What days/times would you be available to work on research?

References (At least one should be a professor/instructor, if possible):

Name _____ Phone _____ Relation _____

Name _____ Phone _____ Relation _____

Please return to Dr. Milevsky, OM 390 or fax it to 610-683-4467.

FIGURE 5.2 Sample application.

If this happens, you can then upgrade students from your second tier and invite them to join the project.

Once you have commitments from the students you want, separate the students you are not currently interested in into two groups: those who definitely do not make the cut and those who may be considered in the future. Email a nicely worded rejection letter to the former group and let the latter group know that you have filled all the spots you need currently but they are welcome to contact you in a future semester to see if there is an opening on the project.

The "Open Door" Model

The second approach to the selection process is what we call the "open door" approach. In this model, you allow all interested students to join the project. As soon as they reach out to you expressing some interest invite them to a group meeting and get them working. The basic idea is to let the interest level of the students serve as a self-selection mechanism. You should still seek to raise students' interest in your project in various ways, but, having made your best efforts, you then allow the "cream to rise to the top," as it were.

When students respond to your recruitment efforts, many will approach you quite tentatively. They often assume that you are going to be selective and they want to know what qualifications they need to join your project. Probably the most frequent question will be, "How much time do I have to devote to the work and during what exact times?" Often, from your point of view, the most important qualification is an intense interest in getting involved in this new experience. Students who are serious about benefiting from the experience will make time for it. Those who are less serious (which they may not find out until they try) will drop out. In some situations, this is a benefit, not a problem. It enables you to accurately identify the students who will contribute the most to your program without having to invest any of your resources in developing and implementing a selection process.

It is typical that by the end of the first few weeks of a semester as many as two dozen students will have expressed interest in joining your project. The least interested students will drop out quickly. Then there will be a core that begins regular attendance at your weekly lab meetings (more about strategies for lab meetings later). As you orient them to your projects, you will announce the various needs that you see arising and you will solicit volunteers. Some of these needs will be more demanding in terms of time commitment, others less. Some of them will require a commitment of more specific times at specific places, such as running subjects or interviewing participants. Others will be much more flexible with regard to how fast the task is completed and where the work can be done, such as coding data or working on developing new stimulus or survey materials.

The students' responses to these needs will be another part of the selection mechanism. But here, by selection I mean determining which students can help you best at what tasks. It is often to your advantage to stress that you are not judgmental about how much time students devote to your project. You can say that you are perfectly willing to accept the help of a student who can only work a little bit here and there on a very flexible task. If the task progresses too slowly, there will probably be other students in similar positions who can lend a hand. By making use of several such students it is often possible to get a lot of work done. For example, it may seem to you that hand coding a box full of raw data is going to be a long, tedious, and onerous task. But two or three students working whenever they can on a flexible schedule will often knock off such a task in a surprisingly short time. You may actually find that using student labor in this way puts you in the position of being pressured to keep up with them. So, as you can see, you should not risk making students reluctant to volunteer for a task because they think you will be unhappy if they do not devote enough time to it. Doing so could cost you the loss of some valuable student labor. More importantly, it could cost those students the loss of an opportunity to start getting involved—a beginning that could lead to an increase in interest with subsequent greater involvement and greater benefits.

The general policy for the "open door" policy, then, should be to encourage as many students as possible to at least take a shot at getting involved. You never know when there may be a student out there who might be very tentative at first, but who might turn out to be very beneficial to your program, and who might, in turn, benefit greatly from it.

Motivating and Managing Research Assistants

There are many possible approaches to motivating and managing research assistants, and which one works best might depend on whether you favor the "exclusive club" model, or the "open door" approach. Assuming you have determined that the "exclusive club" model will work best for you, consider the following.

Group Sub-Teams

Once you have a core of committed students on your research team you must work continuously on managing and motivating the students. Depending on the number of students you have, you may want to set up sub-teams, each with its own team leader, charged with different aspects of the work. Table 5.1 provides several examples of sub-team responsibilities.

Your team leader should be chosen very carefully. The last thing you need is research group politics triggered by your selection (although research group politics is a sign of strength; it shows that your students are committed to, and are concerned for, the project). Selection based on seniority is your best option, unless the senior members of your team are not the most qualified.

TABLE 5.1 Examples of Team Responsibilities

Title	Responsibilities
Lab organizer	If your group has lab space the organizer can oversee the physical setup of the laboratory space.
Web page development	A tech-savvy student can be charged with developing a web page for your study.
Director of pilot study	If your work required a pilot study to test out a new survey or questionnaire, a student can be charged with organizing the endeavor.
Director of personnel	It is always useful to have a student keep track of personnel and update the staff directory.
Conference organizer	This student can compile and update a list of upcoming conferences to which you plan on submitting including submission deadlines.
Director of data entry	Although this is a general task, someone overseeing the progress can be extremely beneficial.
Library research	Choose a student who is comfortable with library research and have them be the point person for literature reviews.
Public relations	Creative publicity about your work and findings is always a bonus and can attract future assistants.

Student Motivation

An additional challenge that may surface throughout the project is motivating the students. Although students are extremely motivated at the start of their involvement with your project, after several weeks they may begin to find the work somewhat uninteresting at times and may need some extrinsic motivation to continue performing at a high level.

Your motivation efforts should take on elements of other types of team motivation efforts. First, the sooner you can honestly include a student as a co-author on a presentation, the more committed and motivated the student will be. You may even start with having them take part of your data and work on a presentation for a local student conference. Aside from simple positive reinforcement, inclusion as a co-author promotes a feeling of ownership over the project by the student, which fosters a deeper involvement and investment in the project. Second, building a sense of team spirit can be very useful in motivating students as well. A project web page including a project staff page can assist in these efforts. Furthermore, holiday and end-of-the-semester parties are additional useful tools in encouraging closeness between project members.

If you have decided that the "open door" policy would suit your needs best, then some of the ideas suggested above, might be modified somewhat. For example, in the "exclusive club" model you might require attendance at lab meetings, whereas in the "open door" approach attendance at lab meetings might be more flexible. In this approach, it might be emphasized to the research assistants that the more they can contribute, the more they will benefit, but that it is left up to them. This will result in attendance at meetings serving as part of the self-selection process described earlier. It can also be emphasized that attendance at lab meetings is more important early in their experience, when they need to learn about your research projects, but it will be less important later, assuming that they will volunteer to work on projects at which they can work independently. You can even explain that among the important qualities that they could demonstrate, for which they could later be praised in a letter of recommendation, are not only diligence (as illustrated by regular attendance early), but also the ability to work independently with minimal supervision later on.

Regardless of whether you use the "exclusive club" model or the "open door" approach, one important consideration will be careful documentation of the lab meetings. Also, either approach will probably involve tracking the progress of any volunteers who are working independently. Those volunteers will probably keep in touch to report progress, get advice as to how to proceed, and so on via email. Carefully documenting both the proceedings of the lab meetings and the exchanges with independently functioning volunteers will be critical.

One method to consider is to keep minutes of lab meetings and any other important information on a project web page. The project web page mentioned previously can be tremendously helpful in this regard. On it, you can have a page that consists of minutes of the lab meetings. One strategy is to type up those minutes either as the lab meeting progresses, or immediately after. You may wish to do this yourself, or you may wish to delegate this to one of your research assistants, as described shortly. You may also wish to add notes about the progress of the independently functioning research assistants to such lab meeting minutes. The special value of having a record in this particular form is that it is so easily accessible (e.g., you can easily refresh your memory about something even if you are away at a conference). Furthermore, the independently functioning research assistants, as well as any research assistant who needed to miss a meeting that they otherwise would have attended, can easily keep up with what's going on in your research program. Finally, think of the benefit of being able to answer the question of potentially interested students regarding "What exactly do research assistants do?" by simply referring them to the web-based meeting notes.

Research Students and Conferences

There are two significant benefits of taking research students to conferences. First, for the benefit of your research, taking students to conferences serves as a great motivator for the students. The entire process of preparing for and attending a conference is extremely exciting for students. This excitement translates into them being even more motivated to contribute to your research efforts.

Taking students to conferences also helps your research team by creating a group orientation. When research students go to conferences together they develop a group cohesion that further benefits the overall research efforts. It also helps in creating a sense of ownership over the research on the part of the students which further connects them to the research and motivates them further.

Beyond the benefits for you and your research group, students themselves benefit greatly from the experience. First, they learn valuable communication and verbal presentation skills during the actual presentation of your research. It also could offer students a great networking opportunity as they connect with other students and reach out to professors and administrators from universities they may consider applying to for graduate school.

The valuable student benefit from this process also has an indirect advantage for you as you may want to highlight in your yearly performance review your work with students and how much they benefit from your research and from the fact that you've taken them to conferences.

Presentation and Logistics

There are two aspects to consider when talking about students going to conferences. First is the research aspect and second is the trip and conference logistics aspect.

When preparing your research for a conference presentation, students can be involved whether you are planning on presenting a poster or you are planning on delivering a verbal presentation. First, students are able to be very helpful in conducting the literature review that you need in preparation for your presentation. They may even be able to draft the entire paper if they have superior writing abilities which then can be sent to you for cleaning up and finalizing.

With a poster presentation, students can even be the ones that format the paper into a poster design. I have found that some students with unique design talents have created beautiful poster presentations. Students can also be involved in developing the PowerPoint presentation if you plan on delivering a talk. The current cohort of students has superior computer design abilities and they can often create either a poster or a PowerPoint that is truly remarkable.

When you are at the conference you can also have students take part in the presentation. If you are presenting a poster presentation, make sure students have some time where they are standing by the presentation and they are the ones fielding questions about your research. This could be an unbelievably valuable experience for students. In some situations, even if you are presenting verbally, you may be able to have students with superior public presentation abilities actually present a part of your paper.

On the logistical side, once you give students a general overview of what needs to be done in terms of travel arrangements and conference registration, you can diversify the work between your students, each of them having to do some research relating to the travel and conference logistics.

The actual level of involvement that you take in making the arrangements for your students depends on your unique style. I have found that when given the opportunity students are able to take care of their own arrangements, which is a side learning opportunity for the students.

There are also different orientations about the benefits of traveling with students to the conference. Some like the idea of going together with them which further contributes to group cohesion. Others professors may find it a bit burdensome traveling with a bunch of rowdy undergraduate students.

Regardless of your choice, it is definitely a good idea to get together with students at the conference beyond the time you spend together during the actual presentation. Taking them out one evening of the conference to dinner is a great way of fostering group cohesion and developing deeper connections with your research students.

Conference Funding

An additional logistical consideration is how to fund student travel and conference expenses. Many undergraduate institutions have an undergraduate research committee where students who are serving as co-authors on a paper could apply for conference funding. It may require the students to compile a proposal, which includes your paper, and in some cases may necessitate the students to present orally in front of the committee.

A quick search on your university's web page or reaching out to the grants office may help you locate the contact person for such a committee. If your university does not offer such an opportunity, in some cases your department or the dean's office may have some discretionary funding for student conference presentations. An additional funding option is Psychology Club or any of the honor societies in psychology. You can have your students reach out to the president of any of these clubs to see if membership in these clubs entitles students to some conference funding.

It is important to clarify to students that if they pool their resources and share the hotel room and transportation even if they do not receive funding they should be able to attend the conference with minimal expense. Usually students have a considerably reduced rate for conference attendance further minimizing the expense.

Ultimately, taking students to conferences will definitely add to your work schedule. However, in the long run the benefits to the students and the benefits to you and your research will be tremendous. Students come back from conferences energized and motivated which ultimately serve to forward your research efforts in a considerable way.

Summary

Considering that professors at teaching universities often do not have the luxury of working with assigned teaching or research assistants, those teaching at primarily teaching institutions need to think creatively about utilizing undergraduate research assistants. Having undergraduates as volunteer research assistants can offer many advantages and knowing how to recruit, select, and manage these students will enhance you research efforts. Furthermore, teaching universities typically expect faculty to engage undergraduate students in research as part of their educational experience. The trick is to develop a research program to which undergraduates can effectively contribute. The most important principle is to inculcate the idea that a meaningful research experience requires multiple semesters of participation. You can expect that it will take a full semester, at least, just to familiarize undergrads with your research to the point where they can begin to make a meaningful contribution that will be helpful to you and the kind of learning experience that will be genuinely valuable to them.

Suggested Readings

Evans, N. J., Forney, D. S., Guido, F. M., Patton, L. D., & Renn, K. A. (2009). *Student development in college: Theory, research, and practice*. San Francisco, CA: Jossey Bass.

> This book offers a clear understanding of college student development, an important tool for anyone working with this population.

Person, D. R., Ellis, P., Plum, C., & Boudreau, D. (2005). Using theory and research to improve student affairs practice: Some current examples. *New Directions for Community Colleges, 131,* 65–75.

> Written from a career counseling perspective, this article can inform faculty about student success in multiple contexts, including research work, particularly for underrepresented populations.

6

BUREAUCRATIC ODDS AND ENDS

After Reading This Chapter You Will Know How to

- Watch for documents, such as a travel grant application or an IRB application, that could serve as useful templates, so that you can save them for future use.
- Set up a system to record all activities of a research group so that information needed for a letter of recommendation can be easily found.
- Help your administration be more aware of the details of your research so that you are less likely to be denied help simply because they do not fully understand your needs.

Introduction

Some of the bureaucratic tasks that you have to perform as a researcher are things that you have to do yourself. These are paperwork tasks that are aggravating to have to deal with but cannot be avoided. For example, at my institution I can obtain travel funds to present at a convention, but I have to fill out the application. As another example, I need to keep my group of research assistants organized. I have to keep records of who volunteered, when they started, what tasks they have gained experience at, and how long they plan to work for me. The payoffs of being able to present at a convention without spending my own money for travel and accommodations, or of having a group of undergraduate volunteer research assistants to help me, are great enough to motivate me to do what I have to do in terms of paperwork. But anything that can alleviate the burden of that paperwork is very welcome.

Other tasks involve dealing with various entities at your institution over which you do not have any direct control. For example, you need to apply to your Institutional Review Board (IRB) for permission to use human subjects for your research. If you need to take a sabbatical to conduct research, you have to apply to a sabbatical committee. These entities may have entrenched policies that sometimes tend to impede rather than facilitate your efforts to conduct research. You need to work with them rather than against them to get what you want. The reason that their policies seem to stand in your way is not because anyone intentionally wants to make your life difficult. There are reasons for their policies. The members of these boards and committees want to help you, but they have their own responsibilities to attend to in the process. Therefore, if there is some policy that works against your interests, it may be because the people who implement them are unaware of the problem. There might be a solution that helps you and still enables the committee to meet its responsibilities. You might just need to educate them about some aspect of your needs of which they are unaware.

Distinguishing between What Is and Is Not in Your Control

If the bureaucratic stumbling block you face is that there are tasks that you cannot avoid, but that take up a lot of your precious time, then the solution is to develop strategies to be more efficient at those tasks, just as you may need to be more efficient at your teaching. These are things that you can do yourself. However, if the bureaucratic stumbling block involves working with one of the committees within your administration, then solving the problem might be less within your control. When this happens, it might sometimes be because, in spite of their good intentions, the committee impedes your research unnecessarily because of something that they are not aware of, but that you, because you are directly involved in research, are aware of. Therefore, if you can work with the committee in such as way as to tactfully educate them, you may be able to make headway against this kind of problem as well.

Things That Are Within Your Control

First, I will discuss examples of strategies to help you with the paperwork and record keeping tasks that are within your control. Next I will discuss examples illustrating how your administration may need to be educated about your needs in order for you and them to work together better.

The Travel Grant Application as an Example of Paperwork

Consider the example of the travel grant application at my institution. I should be clear that this example is not meant to disparage the people who create or run these systems. There are very good reasons for the complications that result from the responsibilities of their jobs. I just want the reader to be prepared for those complications, and, of course, I'll suggest ways to handle them. And so, regarding the travel grant application at my institution, first, one must be aware that there may be a distinction at your institution similar to that at ours. Specifically, to request funding for your research I have to develop a grant proposal. However, to request funding to travel to present that research at a conference I have to fill out a professional development application, which is an entirely different animal.

Here is how the bureaucracy works at my institution. "Travel Assistance" is Category 4 in professional development. There is a cover sheet for the professional development application. The cover sheet is found on page 10 of the 11-page set of guidelines that can be downloaded from the website of the Office of Grants and Sponsored Projects. There is no Office of Professional Development. But there is a Professional Development Committee.

The cover sheet lists the items that must be included in your proposal (the title at the top of the cover sheet calls it an "Application," but the list refers to the application as a "proposal"). The list includes a "Copy of acceptance letter describing the qualifying role," "Abstract of paper," "Original signed Travel Expense Form" (a completely separate form from Accounts Payable that is obtained from your department secretary, is placed within this application, and gets handled with its own procedure), a "Copy of registration material," and an "Itemization of Costs" (even though all of the costs are on the "Travel Expense Form").

When you fill out the Travel Expense Form, you have to state the costs for your room, your flight, and your meals. To state the cost for your meals you have to go to a government website that lists the federally approved per diem rates for the city to which you will be traveling. You must submit this application far enough ahead of time for it to get through the process of being approved by the chain of command at the university. However, that far in advance, you do not know on which day of the conference your presentation is scheduled. Therefore, you do not know for sure what days of the week you will be flying (which affects the fare) nor do you know what days and how many days you will be attending the conference (which affects the accommodations cost).

As a result, you either wait until you know those things (which is what I did when I first encountered this process), thus risking being too late with your application, or you estimate, and you estimate the highest amount you think you may need. Your institution will probably have no problem reimbursing you for less than the amount they approved, but they will not reimburse you for more. I learned from experience that estimating high is the way to go. You don't risk your application being turned down on the grounds that you are asking for too much because if you ask for more than the Professional Development Committees has allotted for such travel, they simply reimburse you for their maximum, and the rest has to come from some other source. That other source could be out of your pocket, or, as is the case for me, fortunately, my department kicks in the rest of the money.

Once you have all of your documents and cost estimates together, the procedure for submitting the application to the committee at my institution is to send them one original with signatures and seven, two-sided copies. Why two sided? Why seven hard copies? Aren't we in the twenty-first century, in which documents are sent as PDFs via email? Apparently there are seven members of the committee and either they don't like to carry around more pages than necessary in their briefcases, or they are just conservation-sensitive enough to want you to only use up half as much paper as you would have for one-sided copies, but not enough to be willing to read a .pdf from their computer screen.

Perhaps I'm being too hard on my colleagues. As I mentioned earlier, there may be good reasons for the seemingly strange policies of which I am unaware. At any rate, the only point in asking might be to make the administration aware that there might be a better way. Getting changes to long-standing policies that could be improved might be worth the effort, or it might not. The only way to find out would be to bring the matters to the attention of the administration and hope for the best. Meanwhile, if change is not forthcoming any time soon, you still need a way to deal with the policies.

When I first encountered the process of applying for travel funds, I stumbled through it by asking a lot of questions. As mentioned above, I did not at first catch on to the fact that I should be more worried about getting the application in on time than on getting the projected costs exact. I also assumed that once I had done it the first time, it would be much easier from then on. It turned out, however, that for several years in a row, each time I faced that process, I had to ask the same questions again. My judgment that I would remember from the previous year was wrong. Instead, somewhere along the line I, realized that I needed a better strategy.

That strategy was to become a packrat of sorts. In the case of the travel grant applications, I eventually learned that each time I had to do one, the procedures involved would seem just as bizarrely complicated as the last time. The process never got easier to understand because I had done it before. The only way that I could speed the process was to save copies of everything that I did in one year, so that I could refer back to those copies the next year. Instead of having to search for the guidelines online and read them again, I went to a file folder that had a copy of the documents from the previous year. You could also put a note in with them about any of the parts of the process that wouldn't be apparent by just looking at the copies, such as "One original—7 two-sided copies." It could even be just those words on a sticky note.

I should point out that as time goes on I try to avoid hard copies as much as possible and use electronic copies. In that case, instead of attaching a sticky note, I have become accustomed to creating a text file with the information that would have been on the sticky note, and naming the file something that would catch my attention. Sometimes, I would just create the text file, with a name such as "one_original_7_2_sided_copies.txt" and have no content in the file. Just the name of the file would be the electronic equivalent of a sticky note. Of course, for that to work well, you need to organize your files in folders in such a way that not too many files are in one folder. That will maximize the chances that you will notice the "electronic sticky note" when you need to.

I even learned to take a photocopy of the Travel Expense Form with me to the conference in a folder to remind me to save all of the receipts for everything on the form for which I would need a receipt when I turned it in for reimbursement. After doing that several times it became easier to remember to save the receipt for things like mailing my poster to the conference (that's better than trying it carry it on the plane or risking putting it with checked luggage). And depending on how you get from the airport to the hotel, you may need to learn to remember to get a receipt for that as well. If you buy a ticket for a shuttle, they may automatically give you a receipt, but from a cab driver you may have to remember to ask. It may be vital to get all of those receipts because you may be expected to attach them to your Travel Expense Form when you submit it for reimbursement. The policy may be, "No receipt, no reimbursement, no exceptions." The only exception to the "no exceptions" rule might be the costs of your meals because that is covered by the per diem.

The "per diem" is the amount that you are allowed to cover costs such as meals, snacks, and tips. For major U.S. cities, that may be around $70 per day. Be aware, however, that in a major U.S. city whatever the per diem amount is, it will not go as far as you might think it would. If you wish to actually stay within that cost, then you cannot expect to be eating all of your meals at the hotel. Be brave. Try that street vendor's falafel. And if you plan on buying a memento or a gift for someone back home, you're on your own.

Keeping Records of your Research Assistants

The research assistants that you recruit for your research program will change regularly. Even if you keep some for many semesters, it will still be the case that each semester you will probably get some new ones, and some will graduate or leave for some other reason. Because you are so busy with so many different tasks, those semesters will seem to fly by very quickly. You may have regular weekly meetings to help you keep track of everything going on in your research program, but you may not. There may be semesters in which you have veteran research assistants who are working independently. They may even be helping you to train new assistants. Therefore, it may not be as easy to keep track of who is doing what, or at what point in a process they are, as you might think.

One of the most important reasons for keeping records of exactly what your research assistants did for you is to facilitate writing a letter of recommendation. Writing such letters can be very time-consuming in order to do due diligence by reporting accurately what you know about the recommendee. You won't want to rely on your memory. You will need to have comprehensive documentation. Two strategies that I have developed for maintaining good records regarding my research assistants are having a spreadsheet to keep records of who they were and when they worked for me, and having meeting notes to record the details of what they did for me.

The first strategy that I eventually developed, and have used for the last nine years, has been to use a spreadsheet to keep records pertaining to my research assistants. Each row is for one research assistant, and the columns are as follows. First there is a column for the semester and year. In that column, I indicate the semester and year, and then I number the research assistants. The next two columns have their last and first names and their email contact information. The columns that follow were developed over time by experience. Some columns were not there at first, but were added as I realized I needed them. Other columns fell into disuse as I either realized they no longer applied, or were not important enough to keep using. However, when I stopped using a column, rather than deleting it, I simply hid the column so that it would not be in the way, and yet I preserved the records of what was in it back when I did use it.

After the names of the research assistants is "1st email date." That column enables me to be sure of when a student first contacted me to express interest, and how long they had worked for me when I'm writing a letter of recommendation. The next column is labeled "Active?" In that column I can keep track of the times when a research assistant volunteered and tried to help, but at some point had to back off from doing work for me for some reason, and yet did not wish to be dropped because they intended to return to active duty when possible. Next, the "1st email date" column is supplemented by "1st meeting attended" and "1st meeting this semester." This enables me to be very accurate about when the student actually showed their interest by attending a meeting for the first time, and the same for each semester that they remained active. Next is "Project 1" and "Project 2." Because I often use the overlapping independent studies strategy, and because within any study there may be different parts of the project that an assistant could work on, there can be a large number of different things the various assistants might be working on for me at any given time as their primary project. The reason for "Project 2" is that there might also be times when an assistant might be working on more than one task.

Next is "Class status" (that is, 1st Semester Freshman to 2nd Semester Senior). That is followed by "Plan to continue." Those two columns enable me to quickly and easily judge how much commitment I can expect. That is sometimes important when trying to decide which assistant ought to be given what task. If you need to devote a semester of training of an assistant whom you will need to run subjects for several more semesters you will want to select someone who is early in their college career. Just remember, there is no guarantee that their "Plan to continue" (that is, how many semesters they plan to devote to your program) will necessarily be carried out. Judging how likely it is that the assistant will actually continue will require your getting to know them more on a personal basis.

The rest of the columns have to do with whether they (or I) have completed various steps in the process of getting them involved with the research program. For example, there are columns to indicate whether they have verified to me that they are keeping a log (as described in Chapter 5), whether they have been granted permission to access the lab group folder on the network, and whether they know how to access it. Then there are columns to record several other things that I have to do. For example, I have to create a user account for them on the subject pool system, put them on an email list, and have them sign a verification that they have been given the combination to the lock on the lab door, and that they understand their responsibilities with regard to that combination.

The next strategy that I have developed provides me with a record of the details of what each research assistant did for me by keeping research meeting notes. My method for doing this has evolved over time. At first, I kept a notebook in which I recorded minutes of each meeting. However, keeping notes on paper is not nearly as secure as keeping them on a web page. The first technology that I used for doing this was fairly simple. Whenever we had a meeting, I would hold the meeting in a place where I could be working on a computer or my laptop. I opened a web page editor and jotted down the important points as the meeting progressed. (I have been using KompoZer, an open source web page editor that runs on the major operating systems. It is now becoming somewhat obsolete, although continues to work fine for me. With a web search you may find others.) Sometimes that would entail saying, "Hold on while I make some notes about that" during the meeting. But I found that I could make the initial notes efficiently enough so that it wasn't a severe disruption of the meeting. Then, afterward, I would go back through the notes and clean them up. My lab groups' meeting notes from spring 2005 through at least spring 2014 can be found at http://faculty.kutztown.edu/rryan/research/labgrp/index.html.

If you are keeping your notes in some electronic form, whether in a text document or on a web page, one of the most important things you can do is to record the date of the meeting and the full names of each person in attendance. The first time I created a web page for meeting notes, I made one page for the whole semester. I put in a date for each week and put in anchors at each data. Then, at the top of the page, I put a navigation bar of sorts. Really it was just a list of links to the date anchors, but labeled as "second meeting," "third meeting," etc., rather than being labeled with the dates. I also put an anchor at the top of the page. At each location on the page where a new date started, I put a link back to the anchor at the top. This strategy enables you to easily navigate around the page rather than scrolling for long distances. More importantly, once you have created such a page for the first time, it is easy to create a new page for the next semester. All you have to do is make a copy of the previous semester's page with a new name for the new semester. Then, just delete all the meeting notes, but not the dates, anchors, and links. Finally, just change the text of the dates. The reason for having the links in the navigation bar at the top labeled "second meeting," "third meeting," etc. is so that you do not have to change them.

When you are recording the notes for a meeting, each time a research assistant makes a contribution that you may need to remember later for a letter of recommendation, you need to note that contribution with that research assistant's name.

This enables you later to do a search for that research assistant's name when you are writing a letter of recommendation. Just by hitting the "Next" button for your search you can easily trace the history of that assistant's attendance at meetings and contributions to your research program. If you have been diligent in your recording, nothing will be missed.

The meeting notes can be used for more than just recording actual minutes of meetings. I have used those notes to record, for example, when a research assistant has checked in with me via email. As discussed in Chapter 5, there might be times when regular weekly lab meetings are a good idea. But there might also be times when you have gotten your research assistants busy on projects on which they are working independently. However, just because you are not holding regular weekly lab meetings hardly means that nothing is going on. As mentioned above, research assistants may be checking in with you. Or, you may be sending an email to your whole group informing them of some progress that you have made. I have, for example, sent a copy of a relevant research article that had just been published to my whole group with instructions about how it related to what we were working on at the time. The email itself serves as a record. But sometimes I also copy the email into the meeting notes to make finding that information easier later when I need it, via a search as described above. On the other hand, there may be times when keeping those meeting notes becomes a lower priority. Or, you may, as I have been doing recently, begin toying with some other method of keeping the notes.

Most recently, I have begun trying out a new method of keeping my meeting notes. That method is to use the Open Science Framework (OSF), which was discussed in more detail in Chapter 2. On the OSF, you can create a "Project" for your research group. My research group can be seen at https://osf.io/pzvxu/. At this point, the only thing available publicly are three things. There is a brief description of my research program, the correct format for citing that site in various formats, and a list of the activities that have been performed at that site. You can make your research group project either private, that is, accessible only by the contributors (your research assistants) or you can make it publicly accessible as mine is. Then, on that project, you can create other components, such as a wiki, each of which can itself be either public or private. You can use the wiki facility as a way to record your group meetings and activities. I have just begun trying that method, and so the wiki is not yet publicly available. As yet, I have set my wiki to be readable and writable by me, and only readable by my research assistants.

Even though my lab notes Wiki is not yet accessible to the public, just to give you an idea of how they can be used, Figure 6.1 shows you the first (and at this writing, the only) entry.

As that entry indicates, with further development, using the OSF as a means of communication with my research assistants promises to become a very valuable time-saving tool.

> "These wiki pages are an attempt to put the meeting notes for the Ryan Lab Group on the OSF as an OSF project. As a first attempt, I will make them private, rather than publicly viewable.
>
> The members of the lab group will be contributors on the project. For now, I'll give the research assistants read permissions on the project, but not read-write permissions. At least not on this wiki. In the future, I may want to revisit those decisions. It may be best to keep these notes editable only by me, and to allow the research assistants to create a separate wiki page to send information to me, or to the whole group. I'll have to see what works best.
>
> Here's the first informative entry to these notes:
>
> Gage has finished organizing the file folders for the Stats SE Fall 2015 experiment. Someone had put the data we have collected so far, along with the materials that can be carried over from Spring 2015, into file folders and put them in the top drawer of the left-hand cabinet (thanks, whoever did that). Gage moved all that stuff into the set of organized folders in the second drawer down. I think we still need a label on that drawer to indicate what's in it."

FIGURE 6.1 Lab notes Wiki.

Things That Are Not Within Your Control

Research can take many diverse forms, and therefore the practical needs of researchers to carry out their tasks can be greatly varied. At large research universities, where the administration has a great deal of experience with all of the practical problems of facilitating research, they will probably have developed streamlined procedures to handle those problems. However, at a teaching institution, even though there may be a growing desire to have the faculty involved in research, especially for the benefit of the undergraduate students, the administration will probably be less aware of what researchers need. As a psychologist, my understanding of what researchers in other disciplines need to conduct their research might be limited as well. My perception is that, for example, biologists need specialized laboratory equipment and materials. Physicists need specialized apparatus. Geologists need to go on field trips. But they may have other needs of which I am not aware. Certainly, then, someone who specializes in university or college administration, but not especially in facilitating research might similarly be unaware of the needs of researchers in different disciplines.

Administrators might, for example, know that psychologists need human subjects, but they may assume that much of research in psychology is done by survey methods. They might not be aware that psychologists sometimes use equipment such as eye-trackers. They might not realize how much paper and copying facilities will be required to conduct some paper and pencil research. They might not be aware of the growing concern about reproducibility, and thus may not be aware of the desire on the part of psychologists, as well as researchers in other sciences, to foster openness by making their data publicly available to the greatest extent possible. They might not realize that for some psychological studies the resource that the researcher needs most is many hours of labor. Finally, even if they understand that much labor is required, they may not fully understand what kind of tasks that labor is required for, and that those hours of labor need to come from people who are qualified for that kind of task.

Working with Your Institutional Review Board

The Institutional Review Board (IRB) is a good example of a bureaucratic entity that might, from the researcher's point of view, appear as a stumbling block. However, here are three examples of how I and my co-author have succeeded in working with them to our advantage, while respecting their need to live up to their responsibilities.

First, as mentioned in previous chapters, several of my research studies involved using the students in my classes as my subjects. I have already discussed in Chapter 4 how such subjects can be recruited and can provide data while maintaining the anonymity of which students volunteered and which did not. That avoids the problem of conflict of interest between the need for subjects and giving grades. However, another issue that arises is that you need to provide some incentive to motivate the subjects to do the activity from which you gather data. Otherwise, you may not get sufficient participation to get all the data you need. If you are providing any kind of research credit, or extra credit toward the students' grades as that incentive, then there must be an alternative way to earn that credit other than agreeing to participate.

I should point out that in my case I am very fortunate to have had a chair of my IRB with whom I was able to discuss possible alternatives. And, to my pleasant surprise, he pointed out to me that the problem of motivating my subjects to participate was going to be, in this case, very easy. The way the motivation issue was handled in the case of my studies was related to the way they were recruited. My IRB was perfectly willing to allow me to recruit the subjects by asking them for their permission to use their performance on a class activity as data. Notice that this is distinct from asking their permission to have them do the activity. I was allowed to make the activity a required class activity. This was permitted because the activity was no different from what instructors might require students to do as a learning activity even if they were not collecting data. As mentioned earlier, the only potential risk was the everyday risk to the students' self-esteem if they found the activity difficult. And, in this case, the activity was not even particularly difficult. It merely involved trying to learn from examples. My manipulation only had to do with the way the examples were presented or what the students did with them. Because this involved no risks beyond what the students would experience in their everyday lives, there was no problem with requiring them to do the activity.

The motivation for the students to actually do the activity was that they were required to do so as part of the course. The permission was to allow me to use their performance on the activity, anonymously of course, as data in my study. The only motivation for the subjects to do that was that they would be helping me with my research. Because allowing me to use their performance anonymously was no extra effort for the students, it was easy to get their permission. Of course, it was made very clear to the students that I was unaware of who had given that permission and who had not, and that I would remain unaware until after I had submitted their grades for the course.

As mentioned above, I was in the fortunate position of having an IRB chair who was very aware of an important distinction. Some research in psychology might involve some risk of harm, and therefore one would need to be very careful not to do anything in the slightest way coercive. But research on the effectiveness of various teaching methods can be done in such a way that there are no risks beyond those that the student would face just from pursuing an education. However, it might be the case that not all IRB chairs would readily appreciate that distinction. If so, you are now armed with an example to help make such a distinction more clear, in case you need it.

In the first example above, I did not have to do any convincing. In this second example, my co-author found himself in a position that, at first glance, might have seemed impossible to navigate. And yet, because there was a good reason for his request, he was able to have it granted.

Dr. Milevsky's request was that he be allowed to use a passive opt-out consent procedure, rather than the usual opt-in consent, to recruit high school students for his research. In other words, he wanted to send letters home with the students in which the parents would be informed that, as long as their child consented, their child was going to be included in a study, but that they could request that their child not be included if they wished. I have on several occasions asked my students in my experimental psychology classes, when we were on the topic of ethics in research, if they thought such a procedure would ever be considered permissible. Almost invariably, they say "No way!"

However, there was a reason why Dr. Milevsky needed to use that procedure. His research was on the relationships among parenting styles and sibling relation quality (Milevsky, Schlechter, & Machlev, 2011). He needed to include a representative sample of different parenting styles, including neglectful parents. However, if he had used the usual active, opt-in consent procedure, he would have been less likely to get the children of neglectful parents, than children of parents with other parenting styles, in his sample. Therefore, his sample would not be as representative of the population as he needed it to be. Because the study only involved filling out questionnaires, a nonrisky procedure, and because the knowledge to be gained from the study was potentially valuable, Dr. Milevsky believed that the opt-out procedure was justifiable. In addition, he was able to find a previous study (Steinberg et al., 1994) in which the authors were able to obtain the permission of the U.S. Department of Education to use the passive procedure for a similar study. Armed with this evidence, Dr. Milevsky was able to obtain the permission from our institution's IRB to use that procedure.

The lesson from this example is that even if a procedure you wish to use would not be a readily acceptable one because of some risk that is not ordinarily outweighed by the benefits of the research, it might still be possible to argue that it ought to be accepted if there is some unusual benefit from this particular study that would outweigh the risk. In the case of my example above, Dr. Milevsky was able to cite a prior instance that bolstered his argument. But, do not forget, someone had to have been the first to successfully make that argument. Thus, if you were to find yourself in a similar position, and you could succeed in arguing for the special benefit of some otherwise unacceptable procedure in some special case, you might be the researcher who helps your colleagues continue to extend such research in the future.

This third example of how to work with an IRB involves my experience with their changing their application form. I had been a member of my institution's IRB early in my career. However, at that time there was not much research being conducted at my institution, and as a result I only saw a few applications. Later, as is the whole motivation for this book, things began to change. More and more research was being expected of faculty in order for them to be promoted. At that point, I was no longer on the IRB, although a colleague in my department was. I heard from her that there had been cases in which it had been discovered that individuals had been conducting research, usually surveys, but they had been unaware of all the things that they needed to make clear to the IRB when they asked for approval. Thus, the IRB discovered that there were some things going on that they might not have approved of if they had known more about what some of this research entailed. Therefore, it became apparent to the IRB that the application for IRB approval needed to more clearly spell out all of the things that needed to be made clear by the applicant. And so, a new, and more detailed application form was created.

When I first used the form to apply for approval for one of my studies, one of the questions stopped me in my tracks. It was in the section regarding "Procedures Used to Protect the Anonymity and/or Confidentiality of Participants and Records Management." The questions were "Describe how records (e.g., consents, survey, tapes, notes) will be destroyed. If records will not be destroyed, please explain why not. Until records are destroyed, they must be kept in a secure place, accessed only by the investigator, co-investigators or sponsor/advisor." My first reaction was horror. It sounded as if they were assuming that you are required to destroy your data and that they were asking how you were going to do that. I thought, "What researcher in his right mind would ever destroy his data?" Then I realized that the IRB was assuming that the data you would collect would necessarily be confidential information, and information by which the subjects might be personally identified. Of course, if their assumption was correct, then the questions were perfectly reasonable. The problem was that the assumption would not always be correct.

The reason I was so sensitive about this issue was because my research does not usually involve collecting any information from my subjects that would be confidential. And, even though that is true, it is still the case that once all my data is collected, my subjects are only identified by an anonymous subject number. On the other hand, there is increasing concern among scientists in my field and among scientists in general that science should be as open as possible. That is, unless there is a strong reason not to do so, scientific materials, methods, analysis plans, and data itself should all be available for anyone to scrutinize, criticize, and comment on. Thus, except for information that would compromise the anonymity and confidentiality of research participants, or the release of which might compromise national security, one should never even hide data, much less destroy it.

In order to clarify this issue, I had some conversations with the chair of my IRB, and found that we were actually in agreement. As a way of documenting that agreement, I drafted answers to the questions about confidentiality, including the one about destroying records, that would be applicable to my research, and ran it past him. He agreed that it was appropriate, and I have been using it in my IRB applications for approval for any research to which it would apply ever since. Figure 6.2 shows the questions and my answers.

G. Procedures Used to Protect the Anonymity and/or Confidentiality of Participants and Records Management

Records (including consents) must be maintained for as long as applicable regulations require.

1. Explain how data will be recorded (describe any coding procedure). Will anyone besides the principal investigator and co-investigators have access to the raw data or any other form of data (please describe)? How will data be reported if presented or published (particularly important—will identifying information be masked)?
   No identifying information, nor any personal information, will be collected. Subjects will only be identified in the raw data by an anonymous subject number. The subjects' responses will be coded according to whether their solution was correct or incorrect, their method of solution, and types of errors, if any. Initially, no one besides the principle investigator, research assistant(s), will have access to any form of the data. For publication or presentation we will present summaries of the data and, possibly, examples of individuals' work, but with no identifying information. However, if at any later time some other interested researcher requests a copy of the anonymous data, it will be provided to them.
2. Explain any limits to confidentiality (e.g., child abuse reporting laws, individuals besides the researchers who will have access to data).
   N/A
3. If Internet or web-based surveys are being used, describe procedures for ensuring that confidentiality is protected.
   N/A
4. How will data be stored during the study? What will happen to data at the conclusion of the study? (Please refer to the IRB website for policy and procedure on record retention.)
   The data will be stored either in the principle investigator's office, in his lab, or in some other storage facility if the available storage space in the office

(Continued)

and lab becomes used up. If "conclusion of the study" means at the end of the data collection, then that is the beginning of the time when the data will be stored as explained above. However, after the data has been collected it still has to be analyzed and reported. Also, at any time in the future it may be provided in anonymous form to any other interested researcher who requests it.

5. If audiotaping or videotaping is conducted, describe how tapes will be stored and what will happen to them at the conclusion of the study.
   N/A

6. Describe how records (e.g., consents, survey, tapes, notes) will be destroyed. If records will not be destroyed, please explain why not. Until records are destroyed, they must be kept in a secure place, accessed only by the investigator, co-investigators, or sponsor/advisor.

   In regard to consent forms, they will be retained for at least 3 years, as per Kutztown University IRB policy. They will be stored either in the principle investigator's office, in his lab, or in some other storage facility if the available storage space in the office and lab becomes used up. After 3 years, they may either continue to be retained or they may be destroyed, as explained below.

   In regard to raw or coded data, in general, because they are the original source material for creating new knowledge, they could be valuable enough so that rather than ever considering destroying them, the concern could be how to preserve them in perpetuity so that future interested researchers could examine them. This, however, would not necessarily be the case for all data. If data are deemed not to have such value, and if enough time has passed so that there appears to be no good reason to retain them, and if storage space demands dictate that it would be better to destroy them, then they might be destroyed. If that occurs, then the consent forms might also be destroyed.

7. Expected length of time for study to be completed (data collection and analysis)?
   It is expected that data collection will take one semester, although it could extend into another semester. The initial analysis should take only a matter of a few days. However, at any time in the future it would be possible that the study's researchers, or other interested researchers, could wish to re-examine the data and/or reanalyze it.

FIGURE 6.2 Questions about destroying records.

This interaction with my IRB, the chair of which, as I mentioned earlier, is one of the most helpful administrators with whom I have worked, has served to accomplish two important goals. First, I was able to streamline the process of applying for IRB approval by thinking through how those questions about confidentiality and destroying records would be best answered in the case of my research. I saved the application in which I first used those answers in a file folder named "Example IRB explaining procedures for retaining data," so that I could readily find it and use it again whenever it applied. Second, I hope I made my IRB a little more aware of the fact that not all research involves highly sensitive information, and when it does not, there is an important concern about how the records that constitute the actual data should be preserved and never destroyed. In future iterations of this part of the IRB application, I may make reference to the Open Science Framework (OSF) as the place where the anonymous data would be stored and made publicly available. Perhaps, due to my efforts, the next time our IRB application is revised it will make more clear the distinction between information that could make the subjects identifiable, which should be destroyed, and the anonymous data, which should never be destroyed.

Seeing Things from the Perspective of the Sabbatical Committee

As an example, in Chapter 2, I described some research that I had conducted on teaching methods to facilitate learning in my statistics classes. I explained how an automatic search alert had uncovered a paper about a framework, called the Knowledge-Learning-Instruction (KLI) framework, that might be very useful for conducting such research. One problem that I had been having in previous attempts to publish some of my findings was that reviewers sometimes felt that I had not adequately connected my research with previous similar studies. The reviewers referred to this as not "situating the study within the body of previous research." However, the KLI framework provided an opportunity to rectify that problem in future studies of learning in statistics. But in order to situate a new study within the body of research cited in the KLI framework paper, and papers that would undoubtedly follow, I needed to do an extensive literature search and a comprehensive synthesis of that literature. This was a task that I could not reasonably farm out to my undergraduate volunteer research assistants. Even the very best and brightest of them would simply not have the years of background in the literature on learning that would be required for this task. Even if I could find one that could get up to speed by reading much of the background literature with which I was already familiar and then try to take if from there to read the most recent and new papers related to the KLI framework, it would be unfair to expect such an undertaking from an undergraduate who needed to spend time on schoolwork.

My approach to this problem was, looking back, perhaps naive. I prepared a sabbatical application in which I proposed to conduct the necessary literature review, and then design an experiment, or several experiments, which would apply the KLI framework to examining the best possible teaching methods for statistics instructors. I explained how the KLI framework broke down knowledge components, learning events, and instructional events into categories based on a wealth of previous research in cognitive science. I explained how the framework proposed that these components might be related in specific ways, but how research was needed to provide empirical evidence about what would work best as instructional methods depending on the nature of the knowledge being targeted. In my mind my application provided a clear and compelling rationale for why many hours of intellectual work was required to sort through all that literature so that it could be used to carefully design studies of unimpeachably strong methodology. I thought it would be clear that this was a task that could not be done by an undergraduate research assistant and that would not be possible for a professor to do while teaching four classes per semester and handling all of the other duties we are expected to handle, such as academic advising and working on departmental committees. But, as I said at the beginning of this paragraph, I was perhaps naive, and, at any rate, I was wrong. My sabbatical request was denied.

In speaking to one of the members of the sabbatical committee, he explained that my colleagues from other disciplines quickly dismissed the idea of "simply designing an experiment" as an appropriate justification for a sabbatical. On the other hand, actually conducting the research might be considered a sufficient justification. He used the example that geologists sometimes take sabbaticals to travel to a site that might be the only place where they could examine a particular geological formation. But the geologist would plan the trip and what they would do on it on their own time. I mentioned to him that there is an increasing awareness that psychologists often run experiments that do not have very high statistical power. That results in running multiple small experiments in order to get a statistically significant result, but doing so increases the probability that a statistically significant result occurs only by chance. The remedy being proposed is that psychologists need to run experiments with higher power, requiring not only good controls, but larger numbers of subjects. Thus, an experiment that would be likely to be looked on favorably in psychological circles would be one that had very carefully implemented controls and a large number of subjects. That would require that someone with experience should be the person running that large number of subjects. Thus, such a well designed study might require a sabbatical to run it. He agreed.

Of course, it takes over a year to compose a sabbatical application, submit it to the committee, wait while they examine all of the applications for that year, and then get the results. In that time, I had spent at least as much time as I could on examining as much of the literature as possible that was relevant to pursuing this line of research. I had even engaged my undergraduate research assistants to help me as much as they were able. Although I would have been happier if I had been able to put more of my labor into this effort, my research assistants and I were able to come up with what appeared to be a creditable idea for an experiment to tackle one small piece of the puzzle we were trying to unravel. So now, I was ready to try again.

I prepared another sabbatical application. Notice that this aspect of building my research program was not accomplished in weeks or even months. As mentioned earlier, it takes the patience to be willing to stay focused on an objective even for several years, if that is what it takes, in order to eventually accomplish what you wish to accomplish. This sabbatical application focused on why the amount of labor required was due to the need to run a large number of subjects.

That was necessary in order to achieve high statistical power, and achieving that would make the experiment capable of producing results interpretable as empirical evidence even if the results were not statistically significant. I made sure that I carefully explained to my audience, colleagues who might not be knowledgeable regarding how statistical inference works, that with low power, only a statistically significant result is interpretable. With low power, if the result is not statistically significant, then the experiment is looked at as a failure because no interpretation is possible. But with high power, first, as with low power, a statistically significant result can be interpreted as evidence that there really is an effect of the experimental manipulation. But when power is high, then a result that is not statistically significant, instead of being interpreted as no evidence either way, can be interpreted as showing that there really is no effect, or at least not one large enough to be detectable, even with the high power.

In that sabbatical application, I was able to argue that many hours of labor from an experienced person was what was required to conduct the experiment. Part of why I was able to make that argument was because I already had many years of experience running subjects. Therefore, I know such things as how long it would take to run the specified procedure. I could also say from experience what would be a reasonable number of subjects to be able to run in a day. I was able to argue that the need for good controls required that subjects be run one at a time, or at most two at a time, but not in larger groups. All of this could be seen to require many hours of labor, and hours that had to be put in by a person experienced enough to implement all the controls. Thus, those hours needed to be put in by an experienced researcher, not an undergraduate research assistant. Apparently it was much easier for my colleagues who were not in psychology to visualize that process as actual work that required sabbatical time than to visualize reading papers and thinking about their implications as actual work. At any rate, this time the application succeeded.

Summary

When there are applications to be filled out that involve complex procedures, a good strategy is to save a copy of an instance in which you have successfully navigated the complexities to use as a template for future instances of being faced with the same procedure. Be sure to store it in a file or folder with a name that will readily come to mind the next time you face that particular challenge. If a record, such as the record of your meetings with your research assistants, will contain information that you will need later for some specific purpose, such as for writing a letter of recommendation, then always create those records using terms that will readily come to mind when you need to use the information for that purpose. For example, in your research meeting notes, any time a research assistant makes a contribution to your research program that you might want to use as an example in a letter of recommendation, be sure to note that contribution with the research assistant's full name.

When you need to deal with a committee from whom you are asking for some resource for your research, whether permission to run human subjects, or sabbatical time to move your research program forward, you need to recognize that they may not understand your research needs as well as you would like. In this case, you must remember that they are counting on you to inform them of details about your research, of which they might not be aware, but that can constitute a viable reason for something that you are requesting. Your administration may have good intentions of trying to help you with your research, but they have to balance your needs against other priorities for which they are also responsible. Therefore, as with other aspects of a successful research program, such as building your research team, and getting multiple overlapping projects running, one has to be patient when trying to change entrenched bureaucracies. But with sustained and persistent effort it will all pay off in the end.

Suggested Readings

Birnbaum, R. (1988). *How colleges work: The cybernetics of academic organization and leadership* (1st edition). San Francisco, CA: Jossey-Bass.

> This book explains how the way colleges work is based on the perceptions of administrators, and it offers ways to view the organization in different ways in order to deal with problems more effectively.

Chastain, G., Landrum, R. E. (Eds.) (1999). *Protecting human subjects: Departmental subject pools and institutional review boards.* Washington, DC: American Psychological Association.

> This book provides an overview of the use of human subject pools and how IRBs oversee them. It offers suggestions for improving their functions so as to observe ethical requirements while fostering productive research.

References

Milevsky, A., Schlechter, M. J., & Machlev, M. (2011). Effects of parenting style and involvement in sibling conflict on adolescent sibling relationships. *Journal of Social and Personal Relationships, 28*(8), 1130–1148.

Steinberg, L., Lamborn, S. D., Darling, N., Mounts, N. S., & Dornbusch, S. M. (1994). Over-time changes in adjustment and competence among adolescents from authoritative, authoritarian, indulgent, and neglectful families. *Child Development, 65*(3), 754–770.

AUTHOR INDEX

INDEX